Arthur Avalon

Studies in Mantra Shastra

Part 1

Arthur Avalon

Studies in Mantra Shastra
Part 1

ISBN/EAN: 9783337830205

Printed in Europe, USA, Canada, Australia, Japan

Cover: Foto ©Andreas Hilbeck / pixelio.de

More available books at **www.hansebooks.com**

STUDIES

IN

MANTRA SHÂSTRA

PART I

(Causal Shaktis of the 'Pranava, Kalâs of the Shaktis,
The Tattvas)

BY

ARTHUR AVALON

(Reprinted from the " Vedanta Kesari ")

Printed by
Thompson & Co., at the " Minerva " Press,
33, Popham's Broadway, Madras.

STUDIES IN THE MANTRA SHÁSTRA

(CAUSAL SHAKTIS OF THE PRANAVA.)

BY

ARTHUR AVALON.

It is natural, given the difficulties of the subject and the mystery which surrounds it that strangers to India should have failed to understand Mantra. They need not, however, have then (as some have done) jumped, to the conclusion that it was "meaningless superstition." This is the familiar argument of the lower mind which says "what I cannot understand can have no sense at all." Mantra *is*, it is true, meaningless to those *who do not know its meaning*. But there are others who do and to them it is not "superstition." It is because some English-educated Indians are as uninstructed in the matter as that rather common *type* of Western to whose mental outlook and opinions they mould their own that it was possible to find a distinguished member of this class describing Mantra as "meaningless jabber." Indian doctrines and practice have been so long and so greatly misunderstood and misrepresented by the foreigner that it has always seemed to me a pity that those who are of this Punyabhûmi should, through misapprehension, malign without reason anything which is of their own. This does not mean that they must accept what is in fact without worth because it is Indian but they should at least first understand what they condemn as worthless.

When I first entered on a study of this Shástra I did so in the belief that India did not contain more fools than exist amongst other peoples but had on the contrary produced intelligences which (to say the least) were the equal of any elsewhere found. Behind the unintelligent practice which doubtless to some extent exists amongst the multitude of every faith I felt sure there must be a rational principle, since men as a whole do not continue throughout the ages to do that which is in itself meaningless and is therefore without result. I was not disappointed. The Mantra Shástra, so far from being rightly described as "meaningless superstition" or "jabber," is worthy of a close study which, when undertaken, will disclose its value to minds free from superstition, of metaphysical bent, and subtly-seeing (*Sûkshmadarshin*). A profound doctrine ingeniously though guardedly set forth is contained in the Tantras of the Mantra Shâstra or Âgamas. This is an auspicious time in which to open out the secrets of this Âdhyâtmik science. For here in this country there has been a turn in the tide. The class of Indian who was wont to unite with the European critic of his motherland in misunderstanding and misrepresenting her thoughts and institutions, is to Her good fortune gradually disappearing. Those who are recovering from the dazzle produced on its first entrance by an alien civilization are able to judge aright both its merits and defects as also to perceive the truth of the saying of Schiller " Hold to your native land for your strength comes from it." Ans vaterland ans teure schliess dich an. Da sind die starken wurzeln deiner Kraft. Again in the West there is a movement away from the materialism which regarded that alone as " real" which is gross sensible matter ; and towards that standpoint whence it is seen that thought itself is a thing which is every whit as real as any external object. Each is but an aspect of the one conscious Self whence both mind and matter proceed. This Self or Chit is the Soul of the universe, and the universe is Chit which has become its own object. Every being therein is consciousness that is Chit manifesting as the multiple forms of mind and matter which constitute the universe. This Western movement is called by its adherents " New Thought" but its basal principles are as old as the Upanishads which proclaimed that all was Feeling-consciousness (Chit) and therefore what a man thought that he became. In fact thought counts for more than any material means whatever. I am not however here entering upon a general defence of so immense a subject for this cannot be compassed in an article such as this. The present note is but a short summary of the result of some enquiries recently pursued in Kashmir with a view to ascertain the notions of the Northern Shaiva school on several matters which I had been studying in connection with an intended work on the wakening of the spiraline energy or Serpent Power. I was already aware, as the Kulârnava Tantra (one of the foremost Tantras of the " Bengal" school) indicates, that the Shaiva-shâkta Darshana and not Shangkara's exposition of Vedânta is the original philosophical basis of the Shâkta faith though some who call themselves Shâktas seem nowadays to have forgotten if they were ever aware of that fact. In Kashmir, Kula Shâstra is, I believe, another name for the Trika. But amongst several other objects in view I wished to link up the connection of certain Shaktis mentioned in the Kriyâ portion of the Shâstras with the thirty-six Tattvas of the Shaiva-shâkta school, their position in the scheme not being in all cases clear to me according to the information previously at my disposal. I have worked the matter out in more detail in the work which is now in the press, but the present article will summarise conclusions on certain points.

Being (Sattâ) is of two kinds, formless (Ârûpa), and with form (Rûpa.) In the first the "I" (Aham) and the "This" (Idam) or universe representing the Prakâsha and Vimarsha aspects of experience are one. Shiva and Shakti exist in all the planes. But they are here undistinguishably one in the embrace of the Lord (Shiva) and "the Heart of the Lord" (Shakti). Shiva is Chit. Shakti is Chidrûpinî. He is Para and She Parâ. This is the Perfect Experience which is Ânanda or "Resting in the Self" (Svarûpavishrânti). Shiva then experiences the universe as Parâshakti that is Parânâda and Parâvâk. This is the love of the Self for the Self. The Supreme experience is the bliss of unalloyed Love. The Idam then exists as Parâshakti. The two aspects are as it were one (Ekam tattvam iva) to use a phrase in the Ahirbudhnya Samhitâ of the Pâncharâtra Âgama. The "Supreme Sound" and "Supreme Speech" are thus the perfect Universe which is the supreme Kailâsa. This is the supreme unitary experience in which, though the "I" and the "This" do not cease to exist, they are both in their Svarûpa and thus mysteriously coalesce in one, unity of Being which is the "Two in one." The whole process then of creation, that is the rise of imperfect or dual experience, is the establishment through the negation of Shakti (nishedha-vyâpârarûpa-shakti) of a diremption in the one unitary consciousness whereby the Aham and the Idam which had then existed, coalesced in one, diverge in consciousness until in our own experience the "I" is separated from the "This" seen as objects outside ourselves.

The process of manifestation of Mantra is that of cosmic ideation (Srishtikalpanâ) in which Jnâna Shakti first merely formulates as thought the outlines of the limited universe which is about to emerge from and for consciousness, and which is called the "thinkable" (mantavya) which through Nâda which is Kriyâshaktirûpa moves towards the "speakable" (Vâchya) with which again consciousness identifies itself as Bindu which is characterised by a predominance of activity (Kriyâprâdhânyalakshana). Diversity (Prithag-bhâva) is then produced by Bindu as Makâra in the Mâyâ Tattva. Shakti as Ukâra creates objects (Prameya) as separate existences and by the completion of the Tattvas objectivity is completely revealed as Akâra. To describe however adequately this grand system of Âbhâsa, as it is called, would require a full exposition of the Northern or monistic Shaiva and the allied Shâkta

4

Darshana on which the Shâkta doctrine and practice of the Agamas
is based. I can here only indicate shortly the Shaktis of the Mâla
Mantra or Pranava which are the cosrespondences from the Shakti
aspect of the Shaiva-Shâkta Tattvas. The accounts of the Shaktis
vary but such variance is rather due to the fact that some accounts
are fuller than others than to any substantial difference in principle.

The gist of the matter may be shortly stated as follows :—In
creation, the three Shaktis, Jnâna, Ichchhâ, Kriyâ, manifest. These
are manifested powers of the supreme Bindu. " What is here is
there," and these Shaktis of the Lord (Pati) appear as the Gunas of
Prakriti in the Pashu ; or as it has also been said Jnâna and Kriyâ
with Mâyâ as the third appear as Sattva, Rajas, and Tamas of the
Purusha-Prakriti stage which is the immediate source of the consciousness of the Pashu. Svânga-rûpeshu bhaveshu patyurjnânam
kriyâ cha yâ Mâyâtritiye te eva pashoh sattvam rajas tamah (Ishvara
Pratyabhijnâ IV 1, 4.) The creative consciousness (Shakti) projects
the universe as all-diffusive Consciousness (Sadâkhya Tattva) which
considered from the mantra aspect is all-diffusive " Sound," that is
movement or Nâda. Here the emphasis is on the Aham, which is
yet coloured by the Idam as the universe faintly rises into the field of
the changeless consciousness. Consciousness then identifies itself
with the clearly perceived Idam and becomes Bindu. Here the
emphasis is on the Idam with which consciousness becomes a point
(Bindu). Then the evolving consciousness holds the " I" and the
" This" in equal balance (Samânâdhikarana) at which point Mâyâ
Shakti, which is the sense of difference (Bhedabuddhi), intervenes
to separate the Aham (as Purusha) and Idam (as Prakriti) hitherto
held as parts of the one Consciousness and the divisive power of
Kalâ Shakti breaks up the universe so separated from the Self into
that plurality of objects which is our ordinary worldly experience.
The universe which in the Purusha Prakriti stage was seen as a
whole though different from the Self is now also seen as separate
but as a multitude of mutually exclusive beings.

There is first a fivefold division of the " five rays " of Om,
namely, A, U, M, Nâda, Bindu, Shânta. The Prapanchasâra Tantra
says that Jâgrat is Bîja, Svapna is Bindu, Sushupti is Nâda, Turîya
is Shakti and the Laya beyond is Shânta. This is the simplest
form of statement setting forth one Shakti for each of the Varnas,
and the Chandra-Bindu. In other words from Shiva-Shakti
(which includes all the Tattvas down to the appearance of the
three Devatâs) these latter are produced. There is next a sevenfold division. Parâsamvit or Paramashiva is not technically
accounted a Tattva, for the Supreme Experience is Tattvâtîta,

But if we include it as the transcendental aspect of the Shivatattva from which the Ābhāsa proceeds we get the number seven counting Purusha and Prakriti as two. The number seven is of frequent occurrence; as in the case of the seven Shivas, namely, Parashiva, Shambhu and the five Mahāpretas; the seven Shaktis of the Ongkāra as given in the Shāradā Tilaka; the seven Shaktis Unmani and the rest as given in the Commentary of Kālīcharana on the Shatchakranirūpana chapter of Pūrnānanda Svāmī's work entitled Shrītattvachintāmani published as the second volume of my Tantrik Texts; and the three and a half coils of Kundalini of which the Kubjikā Tantra speaks namely Purusha, Prakriti, Vikriti, which it may be observed when uncoiled and divided by its diameter gives seven divisions.

The Shāradā speaks of six Shaktis which with the Parameshvara who is Sachchidānanda make seven namely :—Shiva, Shakti, Nāda, Bindu (Kārana), Bindu (Kāryya), Nāda (Kāryya) and Bīja. The other seven Shaktis above mentioned are Unmani (or Unmanā) Samani (or Samanā) Anjī, Mahānāda (or Nādānta), Nāda, Ardhachandra and Bindu. If in the first series we take Kāryya Nāda which is described as the Mitha samavāya (mutual relation) of Shivarūpakāryya Bindu and Bīja which is Shaktirūpa as the correspondence in this scheme of the Shaiva Shuddhavidyā Tattva with its Samānādhikarana then this series represents all the Shaiva Tattvas up to and including Purusha-Prakriti. The same remarks apply to the second series of Shaktis or causal forms (Kāranarūpa). The first is described by Kālicharana as the state in which all mindness (Manastva) that is ideation ceases. Here there is neither Kalā nor Kāla for it is "the sweet pure mouth of Rudra" (Shivapada). The second is the cause of all causes (Sarvakāranakāranam). The third which is also called by him Vyāpikā Shakti appears in the beginning of creation. Mahānāda is the Kārana Nāda which is Kriyā Shakti and the first appearance of Nāda. Shakti as Nāda is a development of the latter which is transformed into Ardhachandra and then Bindu.

These Shaktis (as well as two others with AUM, making together twelve) are explained according to Shaiva views in an account extracted from the Netra Tantra with Kshemarāja's Commentary and from the Tantrāloka. There the Shaktis are given as Unmanā, Samanā, Vyāpikā (or Vyāpini) Anjani, Mahānāda, Nāda, Nirodhinī, Ardhachandra, Bindu, Makāra, Ukāra, Akāra. The Sanskrit passages here given are the summary in his own language made for me by the Kashmirian Pandit Harabhatta Shāstri of Srinagar.

" When the Supreme Shiva beyond whom there is nought, who is in the nature of unchanged and unchangeable illumination moves forth by His will such (willing movement as) Shakti (though in fact) inseparable from Him is called Unmaná. Her place is in the Shiva Tattva (*Anultara paramashiva avichalaprakáshátmá yadá ichchhayá prasarati sá shakti shiváá abhinnaiva Unmaná ityuchyate; tat-sthánam shiva-tattvam iti*).

" When the Unmaná Shakti displays Herself in the form of the universe beginning with the Shúnya and ending with Dhará, formulates as mere thought the thinkable, then She is called Samaná as well as Shakti-tattva" (*Yadá unmaná-shakti átmánam kshobhayati shúnyádiud dharántena jagad-átmaná sphuráti mantavyam manana-mátrena ásutrayati, tadá Samaná ityuchyate, Shakti-tattvam iti cha*). "This Samaná Shakti Herself is called Vyápiní when She operates as the Power which withdraws into Herself all thinkables which are Her creation. She resides in the Shakti-tattva" (*Samaná shaktireva svamantavye samhárapradhánatrena Vyápiní ityuchyate, eshá Shaktitattve tishthati*). "It is again the same Samaná Herself who is called Shakti when Her operation is chiefly creative in regard to Her own thinkables. She resides in the Shakti-tattva and is also called Anjaní because of Her being coloured (by association) with the thinkables' (*Samanaiva svamantavye srishti-pradhánatvena shaktirityuchyate eshá Shakti-tattve tishthati mantavyoparaktatvát cha Anjaní ityapi uchyate*). " When Shabdabrahman moves forth with great strength from Its Shiva form then the very first sound (produced thereby) like the vibration produced by a sounding bell is called Nádánta (*i.e.*, Maháńáda). It resides in the Sadáshivatattva." (*Yadá shabdabrahma shivarúpáá ativegena prasarati tadá prathamataram ghántánurananátmá shabdo Nádántah ityuchyate, sa Sadáshtva-tattve tishthati*). " When Shakti fills up the whole universe with Nádánta then She is called Náda. And this also is the Sadáshiva Tattva because of the equality therein of the "I" and the "This" (*Nádántena yadá vishvam ápúrayati tadá Nádah ityuchyate, sa cha ahautedantayoh · sámáuyádhikaranyena Sadáshiva-tattvam iti*). Samánádhikarana in its technical sense is the function of the latter developed Shuddhavidyá Tattva. Apparently its original is here represented to be the function of the earlier Sadáshiva Tattva in which the duality of the Aham and Idam first manifests.

When Náda after having ceased to operate in its universal scope, does so limitedly 'or particularly) then it is called Nirodhiní. This Shakti rests in the Sadáshiva Tattva (*Nádo yadá asheshavyáptim nimajjya adharam vyáptim unmajjayati tadá Nirodhiní ityuchyate sd̂ Sadâshivalattvam âlambate).* "When Nâda is slightly operative towards the creation of the "speakable" it is called Ardhachandra which, is in Îshvara Tat'va. *(Nâdo yadâ îshat vâchyonmesham shrayati tadâ .Ardhachandra ityuchate Ishwaratattve.)* Then "Parâ-Shakti Herself is called Bindu when She is in the nature of inseparate illumination in regard to the whole range of the speakable" *(Paraivâ shaktih yadâ samastavâchye abheda-prakâsha-rupatâm grihnâti tadâ binduh ityuchyate, sâ Ishvara tattve tishthati).*

Makâra or Rudra Devatâ is defined :—"When Bindu causes diversity to manifest it is called Makâra and It moves in Mâyâ Tattva" *(Yadâ binduh prithag-bhâvam âbhâsayati tadâ makâra ityuchyate, sa cha Mâyâtattve)* "When Shakti creates objects as separate existences then She is called Ukâra. It resides in the Prakriti Tattva" *(Yadâ prameyam prithag-bhâvena un-neshnyati tadâ Ukâra ityuchyate, sa cha Prakriti-tattve tishthati)* "When the creation of the Tattvas has come to an end, then because objectivity is completely revealed (Shakti as) Mântri Kalâ (that is the creative art or process considered as "Sound" or Mantra) is called Akâra" *(Tattva-sargasya nivrittiryadâ jâyate tadâ prameyasya pûrnatayâ prakâshanât Akâra iti Mântri Kalâ uchyate).*

The extra five Shaktis enumerated in this account are due firstly to the inclusion of A U M ; secondly to counting Vyâpini and Anjani separately instead of as being the Nimesha and Unmesha aspect of one Shakti ; and thirdly the sevenfold series would appear to include Nirodhini also called Nirodhikâ in Nâda of which it is a more particularised development. Nâda would appear in the fuller series to represent Sâmânyaspanda of the sound emanation. For just as in the region of ideation the evolution is from infinite consciousness to the general and thence to particular ideas ; so from the corresponding objective or Mantra aspect which is that of Shâktopayayoga, motion commences from the unextended point first as general, then as particular movement, at length developing into the clearly defined particularity of speech and of the objects which speech denotes. The rhythmic vibrations of objects is the same as that of the mind which perceives them since both are aspects of the one Shakti which thus divides itself.

Namasî ravaivena tattvâbhidânc.

KALÂS OF THE SHAKTIS.

In the December number I dealt with the causal Sh·ktis of the Pranava. This present article is concerned with the Kalâs. Kalâ is a common term in Tantrik literature for which it is difficult to find an appropriate English rendering. Shiva has two aspects Nishkala (Nirguna) and Sakala (Saguna). The former is therefore without Kalâ. The latter is manifested Shakti as Kalâ. Shiva is never without Shakti, for the two are one and the same, and Shakti in Herself accordingly to Her proper nature (Shakti-Svarûpa) is consciousness or Chaitanya (Chaitanyarûpini). Thus there are said to be no Kalâs in Unmanî which is in the Shiva Tattva. Thereafter with Samanî in Shakti Tattva the Kalâs appear. Thus in Netra Tantra (Ch. 22) seven Kalâs are assigned to Samanî. Shiva is partless but fully manifested. Shakti has parts (Kalâ). But parts as we know them do not exist until after the universe has evolved from Prakriti: that is, parts in the literal sense of the Mayik world. When therefore mention is made of Kalâ in connection with so high a Shakti as Samanî or any other Shakti which precedes Prakriti, what is meant is something which may be best expressed by modes or aspects of Shakti. Kalâ, in short, is a particular display of Power or Vibhûti. Kalâ is also one of the Kanchukas which go to the making of the Purusha consciousness and is the product of higher Shaktis and Kalâs. The Kanchukas or enveloping Shaktis cut down the natural perfections as they exist in the Supreme Self and thus constitute the evolved Self or Purusha. The four Kalâs called Nivritti, Pratishthâ, Vidyâ, Shântâ are specific modes of Shakti well defined. These are explained later. As regards the other Kalâs there is greater difficulty. In the first place the texts are not consonant. This may be either due to inaccuracy in the Mss. or real variances or to both. Then explanations of the terms are in general wanting though sometimes they are given by the commentators. The Sanskritist will however perceive that these latter Kalâs are variant aspects (like Âvarana Devatâs of worship) descriptive of the nature and functions of the Shakti whose Kalâs they are and as such may have been set forth for Upâsanâ ; the lengthy lists being in conformity with the taste of the age in which these Shâstras were promulgated. Thus Kalâs have been called Jyotsnâ (moonlight) and the like on account of their Sarvajnatâdharma that is Prakâsharûpatâdharma ; that which being in the nature of manifestation is white and brilliant as moonlight. So again Indhikâ (kindling) Kalâ is so called because it is Jnânarûpâ or in the nature of knowledge ; and Rundhanî is so

9

called because of its opposing or staying quality as explained later. This great elaboration of Shaktis is also in conformity with a psychological principle on which Tantrik Upâsanâ is based into which I cannot enter here.

The above remarks are illustrated by the lengthy list of Kalâs of the Varnas and Pranava given in Ch. III of the Prapanchasâra Tantra. (See Vol. III of my Tantrik Texts). The Kalâs of Nâda, Bindu, AUM are there given and I will not repeat them here : but I will relate instead an account obtained from Pandit Hara Bhatta Shâstri and taken by him from Netra Tantra which has not been published. The reader of the Prapanchasâra will observe that the accounts vary both as to the names and numbers of the Kalâs. In Netra Tantra seven Kalâs are given of Samanî Shakti, viz., Sarvajnâ, Sarvagâ, Durgâ, Savarnâ, Sprihanâ, Dhriti, Samanâ ; five of Anjanî, viz., Sûkshmâ, Susûkshmâ, Amritâ, Amritasambhavâ, Vyâpinî ; of Mahânâda one, viz., Uddhvagâminî ; of Nâda four, viz., Indhikâ, Dîpikâ, Rochikâ, Mochikâ. Some texts speak of Rechikâ. Niro-dhinî Shakti has five Kalâs called Rundhanî, Rodhanî, Raudrî, Jnânabodhâ, Tamo'pahâ. The Shatchakranirûpana (V. 38) speaks of Bandhatî, Bodhinî, Bodhâ. Rodhinî and Rundhanî, which mean " opposing," indicate the opposition encountered by lower experiencers such as Brahmâ and other Devas attempting to enter into the higher state of Nâda. These Shaktis (like the " Dwellers on the threshold" of Western occult literature) oppose all those to whom they do not extend their grace (Anugrâha) by the Kalâs Jnânabodhâ (wisdom) and Tamo'pahâ (dispeller of darkness). These Kalâs are therefore called Sarvadevanirodhikâ that is they oppose entrance into the higher state of consciousness and they oppose the fall therefrom of such Devas as have attained thereto. Of Ardhachandra there are five Kalâs, viz., Jyotsnâ, Jyotsnâvatî, Kânti, Suprahhâ, and Vimalâ which are said to be Sarvajnapada-samsthitâ. For She is Knower of all. If one can remain in Ardha-chandrapada then all things are known, past, present and future. I am informed that according to Netra Tantra (Ch. 22) and Svachchhanda Tantra (Ch. 20), the four Kalâs of Bindu are the very important ones Nivritti, Pratishthâ, Vidyâ, Shântâ ; which however are said in Prapanchasâra to be Kalâs of Nâda, the four Kalâs of Bindu being there given as Pitâ, Shvetâ, Arunâ and Asitâ. These five modes of Shakti are described later. The number and names of the Kalâs of AUM differ in these several texts. According to the former the Kalâs of the Destructive Rudra are Tamomohâ, Kshudhâ, Nidrâ, Mrityu, Mâyâ, Bhayâ, Jadâ ; of the protective Vishnu the Kalâs are Rajâ (?) Rakshâ Rati, Pâlyâ, Kâmyâ,

2

Buddhi, Mâyâ, Nâdî, Bhrâmanî, Mohinî, Trishnâ, Mati, Kriyâ;
and of the creative Brahmâ there are Siddhi, Riddhi, Dyuti,
Lakshmî, Medhâ, Kânti, Dhriti, Sudhâ. The three Bindus of
the differentiating Parahindu form the Kâmakalâ. The Kalâs
Nivritti and the rest are the generalities (Sâmânya) of the Tattvas
issuing from Prakriti ; that is the Tattvas are sub-divisions or
differentiations of these four Kalâs. Nivritti Kalâ is the working
force and essential element in the Prithivî Tattva or Solidity ; and
is so called because here the stream of tendency is stopped and the
manifesting energy turned upwards. When Prithivî has been
reached by process of evolution and Shakti becomes Kundalî
(coiled ; at rest). Her next movement which is that of Yoga is
upwards by involution retracing the steps of descent. The Prithivî
Anu or point of solidity is inexhaustible potentiality in and as a
physical, that is, sensible manifestation of the Spiraline Power well-
ing up from and coiling round the Shiva-bindu. This aspect of
the Power supplies (as a friend learned in Shaiva literature informs
me) the curving and circular motion which manifests as the round-
ing and spherical skin and flesh with which all Prânî are supplied.
According to the same view Pratishthâ which is the same force in
all the Tattvas from Apas to Prakriti (Tantrâloka Âhn. 10) is so
called because whilst Nivritti supplies the outer covering Pratishthâ as
its name indicates supplies the basis and inner framework on which
the outer physical universe is lain. Vidyâ Kalâ, which is so called
because it is limited knowledge, is the dominant Kalâ in the Tattvas
from Purusha upwards together with five Kanchukas to Mâyâ.
These three are related to the Shaktis Vâmâ, Jyeshthâ and Raudrî
which manifest as the three motions which go to make the universe,
which in terms of consciousness are the movements of the
Antâhkarana towards the objects (Vishaya) of its experience ; such
objects being the combination of lines on various planes, in curves
and circles. The three dimensional framework affords the basis
(Pratishthâ) for the outer solid covering (Nivritti) supplied by the
spiraline Shakti as the manifested sensible and physical. Beyond
Mâyâ there is the consciousness which is peace (Shânti) for it is
free of the duality which is the source of sorrow. The last Kalâ
is therefore called Shântâ and is dominant in the glorious
experience of the Tattvas from Sadvidyâ to Shakti Tattva. Thus
the Tattvas are only the manifestations of Shakti as three typical
forms of movement starting from the kinetic state. It is these
moving forces as the Kalâs which are the inner life and secret of
them. The Kalâs are not dead forces ; for the universe does not
proceed from such. They are realised in direct experience as
Devatâs in and beyond all natural manifestations and may be mad

to serve the purpose of Sâdhanâ. As Divine Beings they are modes of the one Divine Mother worshipped diagramatically in Yantras. As the inner forces in the Tattvas the Kalâs group together the latter into four great "Eggs" (Anda) that is Spheroids comprising those Tattvas only of which a Kalâ is the common dominant feature and inner force. These are the Brahmânda comprising Prithivî Tattva in which all others are involved the bounding principle or envelope of which is ether (Akâsha); Prakrityanda or Mûlânda ; Mâyânda ; and Shakiyânda of which the envelopes are Prakriti, Mâyâ and Shakti, respectively. Beyond all these in the centre thereof and pervading all is the Shiva Tattva in regard to which the Divine Shakti as a Kalâ is an utter negation (Shûnyâtishûnya) an empty space-giving or vacuity producing power (Avakâshadâ) which is the negative pole of the conjoint Shiva-shakti Tattvas. The Shiva Tattva is thus the Paramashiva or Parâsamvit the great Bhairava experience with its supreme experience of the universe negatived.

Regarding then this ultimate Shakti also in so far as it is a manifestation as a Kalâ or moving Power the thirty-six Tattvas of which the universe consists are but manifestations of five forces (Shakti) or Kalâs into which the one partless Divine Shakti differentiates Herself in an infinite variety of permutations so as to produce the universe with parts : namely, Shântâtîtâ or Avakâshadâ, Shântâ, Vidyâ, Pratishthâ, Nivritti.

According to the account given in the Shatchakranirûpana (Vol. II of my Tantrik Texts) and the Commentaries of Kâlîcharana and Vishvanâtha, there is a Shakti called Nirvâna Shakti with two Kalâs which are Nirvâna Kalâ and Amâ Kalâ known as the seventeenth and sixteenth Kalâs, respectively. Unmanî is Shivapada which is beyond Kâla and Kalâ. In Shakti Tattva these have their source. The highest Shakti in this Tattva is Samanî ; Nirvâna Shakti is, according to Vishvanâthâ, Samanâpada or Samanî, the life and origin of all being. (Sarveshâmyonirûpinî). According to Kâlîcharana, Nirvâna Shakti is Unmanî. Shakti as seventeenth Kalâ is Chinmâtra and is called Nirvâna Kalâ. Vishvanâtha identifies it with Vyâpinî Tattva which is Shakti-svarûpâ and above (Parâtparâ) the sixteenth Kalâ. It is Antargatâ of, that is, included within, Amâkalâ just as Nirvâna Shakti is Antargatâ of Nirvânâ Kalâ. *Kâlîcharana identifies it with Samanâ-pada. Amâ is the sixteenth Kalâ. She is the receptacle of the nectar which flows from the union of Para (Bindurûpa Shiva) and Parâ (Shakti). Vishvanâtha cites the Yoginîhridaya Tantra to show that Amâ is Vyâpikâ Shakti. Kâlîcharana agrees as to this. But it has been said by Vishvanātha that Nirvāna Kalā is Vyāpinī Tattva. We must take it then that according to this view Nirvāna Kalā and Amā Kalā are the two aspects, supreme and creative, of Vyāpinī Tattva as Vyāpikā and Anjani. Beyond or more excellent than Amā Kalā is Nirvāna Kalā and than this last, Nirvāna Shakti or Samani in Shakti Tattva where it is bondage (Pāshajāla). Thus Nirvāna Kalā is the Chinmātrasvabhāva or pure consciousness aspect of what in the creative aspect is called Amā, the receptacle of nectar that is the blissful current which flows from the union of Shiva and Shakti. This is the rapture of creation which is known to us also. The same Shakti is in differing aspect Amritakārarūpini as the seventeenth and the receptacle of Amrita as the sixteenth Kalā. Amā is both Srishtyunmukhi (looking towards creation) and Urddhvashaktirūpā (looking upwards that is towards liberation). The former is the meaning of the expression " downward turned mouth" (Adhomukhi). This is the portion of the Petals before Kundalinī ascends.

This is my reading of Texts which are not void of discussion. Thus apart from difficulties in the Text cited I was informed in Kashmir that Shakti is called the seventeenth Kalā or Amā when Chinmātrasvabhāvā ; and Amritā Kalā when Purusha is with the sixteen Kalās which in this case are said to be the Jnānendriya, Karmendriya, Tanmātra and Manas (which includes Ahangkāra and Buddhi). This may be a difference of terminology only. What seems clear is that in Shakti Tattva (of the thirty-six Tattvas) there are two Kalās which represent the supreme and creative modes of Shakti whether we call them Nirvāna and Amā or Amritakārā and Amritā Kalā. The sixteenth is the cause of the sixteen Kalās and the Kalā which is in the nature of ever existent changeless Chit (Chinmātrasvabhāvā) is the seventeenth.

To sum up. Paramashiva (Parāsamvit) in His aspects as Shiva Tattva is the Shūnyātishūnya so called because in His experience there is not the slightest trace of objectivity whatever. Both these aspects are Shāntatīta. Shakti then gradually unveils again the universe for the consciousness of the Shiva who is Prakāsha or the illuminating consciousness which is the subjective aspect of things ; and the experience which is summed up as Shānta Kalā arises extending from Shakti Tattva to Sadvidyā with the Shaktis, Samanī, Vyāpinī, Anjanī and their Kalās ; and the Shaktis of the Nāda and Bindu groups with their Kalās. This is the Spheroid of Shakti (Shaktānda) which is the abode of those glorious Beings who are called Mantramaheshvara, Mantreshvara, Mantra and Vidyeshvara. The Vijnānākalās who are below Shuddhavidyā are also above

Máyá. 'From the unfolding of Bindu the other Spheroids emanate which manifest the three principal forms of movement which go to the m king of the universe. Next in concentric circles arise the Spheroid of Máyá (Máyánda) the field of operation of Vidyá Kalá which is the Shakti producing the limited dual consciousness of all experiencers (Pralayákala, Sakala) below Sadvidyá and in or below Máyá. Lastly the Spheroids of Prakriti and Brahmá provide the vehicles in which the experiencer called Sakala functions. These experiencers comprise all beings from Brahmá downwards who are not liberated. Brahmá, Vishnu and Rudra are the Lords of the spheres from Prithiví to Máyá ; Isha and Anáshrita Shiva of higher Tattvas and lastly Shiva of Shiva Tattva, which is the ultimate source of, but is Itself beyond, all Kalás.

THE TATTVAS.

A knowledge of this subject involves an understanding of the thirty-six Shaiva-shákta Tattvas. Thus it is said that Shakti is in Shakti-tattva, Náda in Sádákhya Tattva, Bindu in Ishvara-Tattva. What then are these Tattvas to which reference is made both in the Shaiva and Shákta Tantras ? Unless these be fully understood, no progress in knowledge of the Mantra Science as here described may be expected.

The Shaiva-Shákta Shástra calls experience by the term Vimarsha. Experience has two elements—the " I " (Aham) and the " This " (Idam); the subjective-knowing aspect (Gráhaka) of the Self and the objective or known (Gráhya) aspect of the Self. For it must be remembered that an object is nothing but the one Self appearing through Máyá as non-Self to itself. as subject. At base the experienced is nothing but the experiencer : though this is not realised until the bonds of Máyá which make subject and object appear to be different are loosened. The " I " side of experience is that in which the Self rests in the light of one's own Self without looking towards another (Ananyonmukhah aham-pratyayah); just as the experience (Vimarsha) which looks towards another is called Idam (yastu anyonmukhah sa idam ñi pratyayah). But this " Other " can only be the Self for there is in reality nothing but the one Self. It is experienced, however, differently. In the Supreme state it exists with the Aham in a mingled union ; in the pure experience between this state and Máyá the " Other " is recognised to be an aspect of

14

the Self; in impure experience governed by Máyá the object
appears to be different from the limited self.

Experience again is, at its two poles, Perfect Experience of the
Perfect Universe and the limited experience of the three worlds of
reincarnation. Between these two extremes there are intermediate
experiences marking the stages whereby the one pure Spirit or
Consciousness involves itself in matter.

The Hermetic maxim says " as above so below." Similarly
the Vishvasâra Tantra says " What is here is there, what is not here
is nowhere." (Yad ihâsti tadanyatra, Yan nehâsti na tat kvachit)
Shaiva doctrine says " that which appears without, only so appears
because it exists within." (Vartamânávabhâsânâm bhâvânâm ava-
bhâsanam antah-sthitavaiâm eva ghatate bahirâtmanâ). " The
manifestation of those things which presently appear, happen in
the form of external things because they exist within." " Therefore
what exists in our experience, evolved from the Supreme also exists
in the Supreme experience though in another way. The Supreme
experience called Parâsamvit is not a mere abstract objectless knowing (Jnâna). It is the coalescence into one undivided unity of the
" I" and the " This," that is of Shiva and the supreme unmanifested
Shakti. The former is the illuminating (Prakâsha) knowing aspect
and the latter that Vimarsha aspect which is " the known." But
here the two are undistinguishably one. This Supreme experience
has the immediacy of feeling. It is Bliss (Ânanda) which is
defined as " Resting in the Self " (Svarûpavishrânti). In the
Mâyik world the Self concerns itself with what it takes to be the
non-self. Here the Universe which is the object of Shiva's experience is the Perfect universe that is Supreme Shakti which is but
another aspect of Himself as consciousness. She is beautifully
called in the Parâpraveshikâ " The heart of the Supreme Lord "
(Hridayam parameshituh). For the Mâyik experiencer (Mâyâ
pramâtri) the universe is the manifested world of objects seen as
different from himself. Supreme Sbiva and Shakti exist in mutual
embrace and love. " Bliss is supreme love " (Niratishaya-
premâspadatvam ânandatvam). The Supreme state is described by
the Brihadâranyaka Upanishad in the words " He indeed was just
as man and woman in embrace " (Sa ha etâvân âsa yathâ strípu-
mângsau samparisvaktau); when there is neither within nor
without, when all thought of lover, loving and loved are forgotten
in the joy of blissful unity. The experience is spaceless, timeless,
full, all-knowing, almighty. This is the state of Shiva without
Kalâ (Nishkala) or Paramashiva. This is Parâsamvit which is
beyond all Tattvas (Tattvâtítâ). This is the Supreme Paradise of

Shiva named Kailåsa. As the perfect Universe it is called Paranåda (Supreme "Sound") and Parávåk (Supreme "Speech"), Parama-shiva is an experience of the Perfect Universe that is of Paranåda Åmarsha paranådagarbhah). Such universe is pure Shakti (Shakti-svarûpa).

Our worldly experience is as it were an inverted reflexion of all this seen in the causal waters of Måyå. Måyå Shakti is the sense of difference (Bhedabuddhi) which makes the Purusha who is subject to it see the Universe in the form of an observing self with a multitude of objects conceived of as being outside of and separate from it. In the Måyik world each self excludes the other selves. In the Supreme experience there is one Self experiencing itself. The Purusha is consciousness, subject to Måyå and the five Kanchukas which are limiting forces contracting the natural per-fections of the Self. Thus the Perfect state is formless ; the world state is with form ; the first is spaceless, timeless, all-pervading ; the latter is the reverse and so forth. Kåla produces limitations of time. Niyati destroys independence (Svatantratå) regulating the Purusha as to what he should or should not do at any given moment of time. The supreme experience is full and in want of nothing (Pûrna). Råga Kanchuka creates interest in objects as something other than the self and therefore desire for them. The all-knowing-ness (Sarvajnatå) and all-mightiness (Sarvakartritå) of the Supreme Shiva are circumscribed through the action of Vidyå and Kålå and the Purusha becomes a " little knower" and " little doer."

The intermediate Tattvas next described explain the process how from the creative aspect of the Perfect Experience the imper-fect World-experience comes into being. Shiva has two aspects in one of which He is Transcendent and in the other Creative and Immanent. The creative (Sakala) aspect of the Supreme Shiva (Nishkala Paramashiva) is called Shiva-tattva wherein is the Unmani Shakti previously mentioned. Through operation in His creative aspect Shiva becomes His own object as the Manifested Universe. For in truth there is nothing else than Paramashiva. Shiva Tattva is the first creative movement (Prathama spanda) of the Unmoving Paramashiva. Shakti-tattva is only the Negative aspect of or in the Shiva-tattva. The function of Shakti is to negate (Nishedha-vvåpåra-rûnå-shaktih.) She who is Conscious-ness negates Herself that is deprives experience of the element of objectivity which is itself as Parå Shakti. There is thus left only the other side of experience which is Prakåshamåtra that is what we should call the " I" (Aham) side of experience when regarded as consisting of an " I" and " This" (Idam). Because in this experience there is no trace of objectivity whatsoever, either of such objectivity latent or expressed as exists in the Supreme or other lower and derived form of experience, the Shiva Tattva is called " the very void" (Shûnyâtishtûnya). It is the experience in which the Self is not looking towards any other (Ananyonmukhah ahampratyayah). The objective content, so to speak, of Consciousness is a mere negation. It is Shûnya because it is empty of objective content. Shakti-tattva is also spoken of as the Will (Ichchhâ) of Shiva as yet Unmahifest and inseparable from Him (Santatasamavâyinî).

This account of Shakti's operation is extraordinarily subtle, explaining as it does how the supreme unitary experience is also the first source of dual experience. Such latter experience and the stages whereby the latter is fully developed can only be produced by positing an aspect in which there is a breaking up of the unitary experience. This is done by first blotting out from the Perfect experience its object or the Perfect Universe (Parâshakti, Paranâda) thus leaving a mere subjectivity. To the subjectivity thus disengaged there is again gradually unveiled the universe at first as unmanifested and then (through Mâyà) as Manifested Shakti. In Parâ samvit the " I" and the " This" existed as one undistinguishable unity. In Shiva Tattva through the operation of the associated Shakti Tattva the " This" (Idam) is withdrawn from experience so that the " I—experience" (Aham vimarsha) alone remains. To this the Idam or Universe is again by degrees presented, when there is no longer an undistinguishable unity of " I" and " This" but an " I—this" in which both though distinguishable are yet part of the Self which eventually through Mâyà-Shakti becomes an " I " and " This" in which the two are severed the one from the other. How this occurs the description of the remaining Tattvas explains. The Shiva-Shakti Tattva is not an emanation because it ever remains the same whether in creation or dissolution. It is the seed and womb of the whole universe.

The first emanation or manifestation (Âbhâsa) of and by Consciousness is called the Sadâkhya or Sadâshiva Tattva. Here it is to be observed that the cause ever remains the same and what it was, though appearing differently in the effect. The Supreme experience changelessly endures even though in its creative aspect it gives birth to the Universe. This Âbhâsa is like the Vivartta of Mâyâvâda the difference between the two lying in the fact that according to the former the effect is real and according to Shankara unreal. This difference again depends on the definition given of reality.

Real evolution (Parinâma) in which when one thing is evolved into another it. ceases to be what it was, exists only in the compounded products of the material world.

In Sadâshiva Tattva there is the commencement of the first subjective formation of ideas. It is called Nimesha (closing of the eyes) as contrasted with Unmesha (opening of the eyes) of the next stage of experience. In the former the Universe as Shakti is seen only faintly. The Self hazily experiences itself as object. It is the first step in evolution and the last in involution. Unmesha is the distinct blossoming (Sphutatvam) and externalization (Bâhyatvam) of the Universe. The "This" (Idam) is faintly perceived by the "I" (Aham) as part of the one Self, the emphasis being therefore on the "I" side of experience. Sadâshiva is He whom the Vaishnavas call Mahâvishnu and the Buddhists Avalokiteshvara who sheds compassion on all. According to tradition this is the source whence the Avatâras come. It is in this Tattva that there is what the Mantra Shâstra calls Nâda Shakti.

The third stage of the developing consciousness is Îshvara-Tattva the externalization of the last. The Universe (Idam) is experienced by the "I" (Aham) distinctly and yet as part of, and not separate from, the one Self. As in the last experience the emphasis was on the "Aham" here it is on the "Idam." This Tattva is called Bindu in Mantra Shâstra and is so called because consciousness here completely identifies itself with the Universe as unmanifested Idam and thus subjectifies it and becomes with it a point (Bindu) of Consciousness. Thus by way of example the mind is completely subjectified and exists for each of us as a mathematical point though the body to the extent to which it is not subjectified appears as an object or extended thing.

The fourth Tattva is known as Vidyâ, Sadvidyâ or Shuddha-vidyâ. In the experience of this stage, emphasis is equal on the "I" and the "This" (Sâmânâdhikaranya). In Shiva Tattva there is the Aham Vimarsha ("I-experience") ; in Sadâshiva the I-this experience (Aham-idam Vimarsha) ; in Îshvara Tattva the Idam-aham vimarsha (This-I experience). In each case the stress is laid on the first term. In Vidyâ Tattva there is an equality of either term in an experience which is that of the nature of the true relation of the Aham and the Idam consisting of a synthesis (Sanggamana) of the two on a single "basis" (Adhikarana) and not on two different "bases" according to the experience of those under the influence of Maya (Mâyâpramâtri) thus eliminating the duality which exists in the latter experience.

3

By equality of the "I" and the "This," experience is in the state of readiness for the next stage in which the two are to be severed. Sadvidyâ as being the intermediate stage between the Pure (Shuddha) and impure (Ashuddha) creation is called Parâparadashâ. It is also spoken of as experience of difference in the form of Mantra. (Bhedâbheda-vimarshanâtmaka-mantr..rûpa). It is experience of difference because the Idam is separated from the Aham. It is the experience of non-difference because they are still regarded as part of one Self. The experience is compared to that of the Ishvara of the Dvaitavâdins who sees the Universe as different from Himself and yet as part of and in connection therewith. " All this is my manifestation" (Sarvo mamâyam vibhavah). The experience is said to be in the nature of Mantra because here we are in the region of pure spiritual ideation. As yet there is no objective manifestation such as exists in our world. Below this Tattva it is said that there were created eight Pudgalas, that is, Jîvas in the form of knowledge (Vijnâna Rûpa) and then seven crores of Mantras and their Mandalas.

At this point Mâyâ Shakti intervenes and divides the Aham and Idam, and the Kanchukas or limitations of the natural perfections of consciousness make it subject to time, space, birth and death, limitation, and desire for objects which it now conceives of as persons and things other than itself. This is the Purusha-Prakriti Tattva. Purusha in Shaiva-Shâkta philosophy is the Âtmâ or Shiva subject to Mâyâ and to the Kanchukas which are limiting forces whereby the Self as Pure Consciousness loses its natural perfections.

Prakriti is the Shântâ Shakti of Shiva in contracted form existing as the equilibrium of the Gunas which are themselves a gross form of the Shaktis of will (Ichchhâ), action (Kriyâ) and knowledge (Jnâna). All things exist in Her who is of the nature of feeling in a homogenous mass. Purusha is enjoyer (Bhoktâ) and Prakriti the enjoyed (Bhogyâ). The latter is at first the barest objectivity seen as different from the experiencing self as Purusha. Prakriti then differentiates into the Tattvas of Mind (Antahkharana) senses (Indriya) and matter (Bhûta) which constitutes our universe.

Purusha does not merely mean man nor indeed any animal. Every single thing in the Universe is Purusha. Thus an atom of sand is a Purusha or Consciousness identifying itself with solidity (Prithivî) manifesting its limited Consciousness as atomic memory and other ways. What Consciousness thinks, that is, identifies itself with that it becomes.

To sum up the Supreme Experience (Parâsamvit) has a creative aspect, (Shiva-Shakti Tattva) which is a consciousness of " I " ·
(Aham vimarsha) which gradually experiences the Universe (Idam)
as part of Itself at first faintly with predominant " I " then clearly
with predominant " This" and then as equal " I and This" ready
for severance by Mâyâ. The latter then cleaves consciousness in
twain thus setting up a dichotomy of subject and object, though in
truth the object is nothing but the Self as its own object. Lastly
Shakti as Prakriti differentiates into the multitudinous beings which
make the Universe. But throughout it is the one and only Shiva
whether as the Supreme Experience or that of the Consciousness
embodied in solid matter. Shakti, Nâda, Bindu mentioned in
previous articles are Shakti Tattva, Sadâkhya Tattva and Ishvara
Tattva here described considered from the standpoint of the
Mantra shâstra which treats of the origin of Shabda.

2 With the Tattvas the Kalâs to which I referred in the previous
article are associated. These are the forms of activity (Kriyâ) of
the Tattvas as Shakti. Thus Srishti (Creation) is a Kalâ of
Brahmâ. Pâlani (Protection) is a Kalâ of Vishnu and Mrityu
(Death) is a Kalâ of Rudra. It is, however, not always as easy
to see the appropriateness of the Kalâs as in the simple examples given. The Shâkta Tantras speak of 94 Kalâs, namely,
19 Kalâs of Sadâshiva, 6 of Ishvara, 11 of Rudra, 10 of Vishnu,
10 of Brahmâ, 10 of Fire, 12 of Sun, and 16 of Moon. According
to Saubhâgyaratnâkara the 19 kalâs of Sadâshiva are Nivritti,
Pratishthâ, Vidyâ, Shânti, Indikâ, Dípikâ, Rechikâ, Mochikâ,
Parâ, Sûkshmâ, Sûkshâmritâ, Jnânâmritâ, Amritâ, Âpyâyini,
Vyâpini, Vyomarûpâ, Mûlavidyâmantra Kalâ, Mahâmantrakalâ,
Jyotishkalâ. The 6 of Îshvara are Pîtâ, Svetâ, Nityâ, Arunâ, Asitâ,
Anantâ. The 11 Rudra Kalâs are Tîkshnâ, Raudrî, Bhayâ, Nidrâ,
Tandrâ, Kshudhâ, Krodhini, Kriyâ, Udgârî, Amâyâ, Mrityu. The
10 of Vishnu are Jadâ, Pâlini, Shântî, Îshvarî, Rati, Kâmikâ, Barada,
Hlâdini, Prîtî, Dîkshâ. The 10 of Brahmâ are Srishti, Riddhi,
Smriti, Medhâ, Kântî, Lakshmî, Dyuti, Sthirâ, Sthiti, Siddhi.
The 10 of Fire are Dhûmrârchikala, Ushmâ, Jvalini, Jvâlini,
Vishphulingini, Sushri Surûpâ, Kapilâ, Havyavahâ, Kavyavahâ.
The 12 of Sun are Tapinî, Tâpini, Dhûmrâ, Marîchi, Jvâlini,
Ruchi, Sushumnâ, Bhogadâ, Vishvâ, Bodhini, Dharini, Kshamâ.
The 16 of Moon are Amritâ, Mânadâ, Pûshâ, Tushti, Pushti, Rati,
Dhriti, Sashini, Chandrikâ, Kânti, Jyotsnâ, Shri, Priti, Angada
Purnâ, Purnâmritâ. Out of these, 51 are Mâtrika Kalâs which
manifest through the Pashyanti, Madhyamâ and Vaikhari stages
(Bhâva) as the gross letters (Varna). Then 51 Mâtrikâ Kalâs are

given in the same account as follows:—Nivritti, Pratishthá, Vidyá, Shánti Indhikà, Dipikà, Rechikà, Mochiká, Parà, Sùkshmà, Sukshamritá, Jnànàmritá, Ápyàyiní, Vyàpiní, Vyomarùpà, Anantà, Srishti, Riddhi, Smriti, Medha Kànti, Lakshmí, Dyuti, Sthirà, Sthiti, Siddhi, Jadà, Púliní, Shánti, Aishvaryà, Rati, Kàmikà, Baradà, Hládíni, Prìti, Dirghà, Tikshnà, Raudrí, Bhayà, Nidrà, Tandrà, Kshudhà, Krodhiní, Kriyà Omkàrr, Mrityurùpà, Pitá, Svetà, Asitá, Anantà. These 94 Kalás are worshipped in the Wine Jar which holds Tàràdiavainayí or the Saviour-Mother in liquid form. She Herself is called Samvit Kalá and so the Yoginïhridaya Tantra says.

Deshakálapadárthátma yadyad vastu yathá yathá.

Tattadrúpena yá bháti táng shraye Samvidam Kalám.

STUDIES

IN

MANTRA SHÂSTRA

PART II

(Shakti—Potency to Create. Nâda—The First Produced
Movement. Bindu—Shakti Ready to Create)

BY

ARTHUR AVALON

(Reprinted from the " Vedanta Kesari ")

Printed by
Thompson & Co., at the " Minerva " Press.
33, Popham's Broadway, Madras.

A STUDY IN THE MANTRA SHÂSTRA.

(SHAKTI—POTENCY TO CREATE).

BY

ARTHUR AVALON.

In my three previous articles I have referred to Shakti, Nâda, Bindu. In this and the two next I will deal in greater detail with each of these three concepts of Shakti. One of the clearest accounts known to me of the evolution of Shakti is that given in the authoritative Tântrik Prakarana called Shâradâ (also spelt Sârâdâ) Tilaka by Lakshmanâchâryya. This work was formerly of great authority in Bengal. Its value is greatly increased by the commentary of Râghava Bhatta. As this work with its commentary is of prime importance—and is cited throughout these articles, I may here note the following account which Lakshmanâchâryya gives of himself at its close. Mahâbala a great sage was succeeded by his son Âchâryapandita, a Deshika (Tantrik) Guru. His son Srîkrishna Deshika had a son Lakshmana Deshika who wrote the Shâradâ Tilaka. Râghava in his commentary called Padârthâdarsha says that Lakshmana was the disciple of Utpalâchâryya who was the disciple of Somânanda, who was the disciple of Vasumanta, who was the disciple of Shrîkantha. This is the Gurupangkti of Lakshmana. His disciple was the great Kashmirian Abhinava Gupta, the author of Paramârthasâra. The latter's disciple was Kshemarâja the author of the Shivasûtra-Vimarshinî. The date generally assigned to Abhinava Gupta is the eleventh century. Therefore Sj. Akshaya Kumâra Maitra, Director of the Varendra Anusandhâna Samiti, who has supplied me with these details of the Gurus and Shishyas of the author concludes that the Shâradâ was written at the end of the tenth or beginning of the eleventh century. Râghava mentions 1510 as the age of his commentary. Taking this to be the Vikrama Samvat we get 1454 A. D., as its date. These details serve another purpose. There are persons who insist on a total disconnection between the Shaiva and Shâkta Tantras. Lakshmanâchâryya was a member of the Kashmirian Shaiva School and his work was as I have stated of great authority among the Bengal Shâktas.

The Shâradâ (Chapter 1, verse 7) says : " From Sakala Parameshvara vested with the wealth of Sat, Chit, Ânanda issued Shakti ; from Shakti came Nâda ; and from Nâda issued Bindu. (Sachchidânanda-vibhavât sakalât parameshvarât asichchhaktistato nâdo nâdâd bindu-samudbhavah). Parameshvara is here Shiva Tattva. He is Sakala, because, He is with the creative Kalâ or Shakti. As already explained Shakti, when Vyashtirûpâ, that is individualised, is called Kalâ. Shiva is always with Shakti. But in the supreme state, Shakti is unmanifest and exists in its own (Svarûpa) form as Being-consciousness-Bliss, (Sachchidânandamayî, Chidrûpinî) undistinguishable from Shiva. Sakala Shiva is thus Saguna Brahman. He is said to be vested with the wealth of Sat, Chit, Ânanda or Being-consciousness and Bliss to show that His association with Avidyâ does not deprive Him of, or affect, His own true nature (Svarûpa). Shiva has two aspects. In one of these He is the Supreme Changeless One who is Sachchidânanda and Sachchidânandamayî. This is Parâsamvit. In the other He changes as the Universe ; change being the experience of the Jiva so created. The cause of such change is Shiva Tattva inseparably associated with Shakti Tattva.

"There issued Shakti." This is a Shakti Tattva of the Thirty-six Tattvas. Shakti evolves Nâda, and Nâda, Bindu. These are aspects of Shakti preparing to create the Universe and are dealt with in future articles Here I am concerned with Shakti Tattva only : that is, with that form of Shakti which is specifically so called; since Nâda, Bindu and the rest are all but names for different aspects of Shakti.

It may be asked how can Shakti be said to issue from that which was already with Shakti. Râghava Bhatta explains that the author here follows the Sângkhyan principle of the appearance of realities from realities (Sadutpattivâda) and speaks of the condition of readiness (Uchchhûnâvasthâ) of Her who being without begining or end existed in a subtle state identified with Chaitanya in dissolution (Yânâdi rûpâ chaitanyâdhyâsena mahâpralaye sûkshmâ sthitâ). Adhyâsa is the attribution of the nature of one thing to another according to which something is considered to be what it is not. In other words during dissolution there is some potential principle in the Brahman which, as manifest, appears not to be consciousness (Chit) but which owing to the absence of operation during the dissolved (Laya) state is identified with Chit. The distinction is very subtly marked by the Sanskrit word Chit for Shiva and Chidrûpinî for Shakti Chit is there in either case, for ultimately there is nothing but Consciousness. But that principle which in creation manifests as seeming Achit is in itself Chidrûpinî. One is consciousness and the other is a principle in the form of consciousness. I prefer to look at Shakti from the Consciousness aspect which is Her own form (Svarûpa) and to say that Shakti in dissolution is what She really is, namely, Chit. In creation consciousness as Shakti has power to veil its own true nature and when subject to this power we attribute unconsciousness to it. The substance in either case is this :—In dissolution Consciousness and Bliss alone is. Then without derogation to the changelessness of consciousness there is an apparent dichotomy into subject and object, that is, Consciousness and Unconciousness. Shakti is conceived as ready to create the Universe composed of Gunas as its effect (Kâryya). In other words, pure Consciousness becomes the world-experience. The Prayogasâra says "She, who is eternal and all pervading, the Genetrix of the Universe issues from Him," Vâyavîya-Samhitâ says "By the will of Shiva, Parâ Shakti is united with Shiva-tattva and at the beginning of creation appears from It just as oil from sesamum seeds when pressed." The Pancharâtra is also cited by Râghava Bhatta as saying "The Parama Purusha at the beginning of creation seeing that She who is Sachchidânandarûpinî is the source (Âdishthâna) of the manifestation of all Tattvas makes manifest eternal Prakriti." These statements like all our accounts in such matters are pictorial thinking, being necessarily imperfect attempts to explain the manifestation of activity of Consciousness.

Cause and effect are really one but appear different. The first aspect of Shakti is its causal (Kârana) aspect. But this again may be analysed into the various stages of its capacity and preparedness to create. These stages are marked by certain names which again are mere labels denoting states of Shakti. Thus Nâda and Bindu are names for those aspects of Shakti which are more and more prone to creation (Uchchhûnâvasthâ). Nâda and Bindu are but two states of Her fit for creation (Srishtyupayogyâvasthârûpau). Shakti Tattva is the first kinetic aspect of Brahman. Shakti then becomes more and more kinetic until as Bindu, Shakti is Ishvara Tattva. This Bindu differentiates into the Triangle of Divine Desire called the Kâmakalâ upon which there is that Brahman Sound (Shabda-brahman) which, bifurcating into Shabda and Artha, are Shakti in its aspect as effect (Kâryya) or the manifested Universe of Mind and Matter. This Tantrik account gives firstly an apparent "development" in the causal body of Shakti being in the nature of a resolution of like to like; and then a real development (Parinâma) of the effects (Kâryya) produced from the causal body. The whole is necessarily described after the manner of a gradual process stated in terms of our own psychological experience. But such a process exists only in time which first appears with the Sun and Moon. Bhâskararâya in his commentary on the Lalitâ Sahasranâma (Verse 117) cites Gorakshanâtha as saying in his Mahârthamanjarî " In a moment the world is created and in a moment it is destroyed."

Shakti Tattva and Shiva Tattva are inseparable (Santata-Samavâyini) the former being only the negative aspect of the latter. Both exist even in dissolution, the first emanation proper being Sadâkhya which corresponds with Nâda in the above mentioned verse. Shiva Tattva is defined in the Tattva Sandoha as follows :— " That beyond which there is none other, moved of His own will in order to create the whole world. The first movement (Spanda prathama) is called the Shiva Tattva by those who know."

Yad ayam anuttaramûrtinijechchhayâkhilam idam jagat srashtum paspande sah spandah prathamah Shivatattvam uchyate tajjnaih.

As the Vimarshinî on the Pratyabhijnâ says—It is the " I-experience not looking towards another" (Ananyonmukhah aham-pratyayah). It is the self-side of experience, Prakâsha or Jnâna-mâtrâ, which is such, because of the negation of all objectivity or not-self by Shakti Tattva. For this Jnâna-mâtrâ She as Vimarsha Shakti provides through gradual stages the objects of its experience. Her function is negation (nishedha-vyâpâra-rûpâ shaktih) of all objectivity so as to produce the mere subjective knowing (Prakâsha-mâtrâ) which is the Shûnyâtishûnya. She then evolves from Herself the objective world in order that it may be the content of the Shiva consciousness. She is pure Will ever associated with Shiva. She is the seed of the whole Universe of moving and unmoving things then absorbed in Herself.

Ichchhâ saiva svachchhâ santatasamavâyinî sati
Shaktih sacharâcharasya jagato bîjam nikhilasya nijanilînasya
(Tattva Sandoha. V. 1.)

She is thus called the Womb (Yoni), or Seed-state (Bîjâvasthâ) and by the Parâpraveshikâ "Heart of the Supreme Lord" (Hridayam Parameshituh). The Yoginî-hridaya Tantra says that men speak of the Heart of Yoginî. She is Yoginî because She is connected with all things both as cause 'and effect. This Yoginî is knower of Herself (Yoginî Svavid). She is called the Heart : for from the Heart all issues. She is the Heart of the Universe : the pulsing movements of which are Herself as Shakti. What

5

more can be said than the words of the Yogini-hridaya "What man knows the heart of a woman, only Shiva knows the heart of Yogini."

In the Pratyabhijnâ-Hridaya it is said, "The auspicious supreme Shiva desiring to make shine forth the Universe existing as one with Himself displays Himself first in the form of the Very Void which is the self-existent Shiva in the form of the experience of the unity of consciousness (that is there is no objectivity) and of undifferentiated illumination (that is Prakâsha or Jnâna). He then next appears in the form of diverse experiencers consisting of an infinite endless number of Tattvas, worlds and beings which are in the nature of a blooming forth of Consciousness and Bliss." (Shrî-parama-shivah svâtmaikyena sthitam vishvam avabibhâsa-yishuh pûrvam chid-aikyâkhyâtimayânâshrita-shiva-paryâya-shûnyâtishûnyâtmatayâ prakâshâbhedena prakâshamânatayâ sphuratî ; tatah chidrasâshyânatârûpâshesha-tattva-bhuvanabhâva-tattat-pramâtiâdyâtmatayâpi prathate).

The substance of the matter may be stated thus :—Whilst from the static transcendental aspect (Parashiva, Parâshakti), Consciousness changelessly endures there is from the kinetic creative aspect (Shiva-Shakti) a polarisation in consciousness, the poles of which are Shiva and Shakti representing the Aham and Idam aspects of experience. Owing to this polarisation there is in lieu of the unitary experience a division into the knower, knowing, and known, Mâtri Meya, Mâna, as it is called. Consciousness then indentifies itself with the products of its own kinetic Shakti, that is with mind as the subject of experience and with matter as its object. This polarisation is explained in the Shâkta Tantras by the illustration of the grain of gram (Chanaka). Under the sheath of the grain of gram two seeds are found in such close union that they appear when held together, as one. With, however, the tearing of the outer sheath the two halves of the seeds fall apart. These two seeds are said to be Shiva and Shakti and the encircling sheath is Mâyâ. Like all attempts to explain the unexplainable the illustration is, to some extent, defective for in the gram there are two separate seeds—but Shiva-Shakti are an undistinguishable unity. The commentator on the Shat-chakranirûpana (Vol. II of my Tantrik Tests) cites the following :—(V. 49). "In the Satyaloka is the formless and lustrous One. She is like a grain of gram devoid of hands, feet or the like. She has surrounded Herself by Mâyâ. She is Sun, Moon and Fire. When casting off (Utsrijya) the covering, She divides in two (Dvidhâ bhitvâ) becomes intent on creation (Unmukhi) and then by differentiation of Shiva and Shakti arises

creative ideation (Srishti-kalpanâ)". By "differentiation" is meant
the polarisation of consciousness into subjective (Prakâsha) and
objective (Vimarsha) aspects. The Self sees another. The same
commentator cites the Prapanchasâra Tantra as saying that the
Parabindu divides into two parts, of which the right is Bindu, the
male, Purusha or Hang, and the left is Visargah, the female Prakriti
or Sah. Hangsah is the union of Prakriti and Purusha and the
Universe is Hangsa. In, however, the Mss. in which my edition
of this Tantra is based (Vol. III Tântrik Texts) it is said that
Parabindu divided by Kâla becomes threefold—Bindu, Nâda, Bîja.
The difference is of no moment for this Bindu (Kâryya) is Shiva
and Bîja is Shakti, and Nâda is merely the relation (Mithah
samavâya) of the two. The combined Hangsah indicates the
same relation as is expressed by Nâda. In the Kulachûdâmani
Nigama (Chap. I, VV. 16-24, Vol. IV, Tantrik Texts) the Devî
says of the first stage " I, though in the form of Prakriti lie hidden
in Being—consciousness-bliss (Aham prakritirûpâ chet sachchid-
ânandaparâyanâ). Then in the initial creative stage when Karma
ripens the Devî in the words of the Nigama " becomes desirous
of creation and covers Herself with Her own Mâyâ." This is the
appearance of the kinetic Shakti. The same doctrine is stated
with greater or less detail in various ways. Unitary experience,
without ceasing to be such, is yet, as Jîva polarised into the dual
experience of the Mayik world. Consciousness as Chit-Shakti and
Mâyâ-Shakti projects from itself, in a manner conformable with our
own psychological experience, the object of its experience. The
Mayik experiencer (Mâyâpramâtrî) takes what is one to be dual or
many. This is the division of Shiva and Shakti which are yet
eternally one. All action implies duality. Duality is manifestation.
Manifestation is nothing but an appearance to consciousness. As
there is ultimately but one Self, the Self appears to Itself; that is
consciousness is polarised. These two poles are the continuity of
the " I " (Aham) and its ever changing content which is " This "
(Idam).

Just as there is absolute rest and a world movement, so Shakti
or Creative Consciousness is itself of twofold aspect, static and
dynamic. Cosmic energy in its physical aspect is potential or
kinetic the first being that state in which the equilibrated elements
of Power hold each other in check. It is not possible to have one
without the other. In any sphere of activity, according to these
views, there must be a static back ground. If one Spiritual Reality
be assumed it cannot be actually divided into two. It is possible,
however, that there should be a *polarisation* in our experience

whereby what is indivisibly one and the self, appears as many and
the not-self. How ? The answer is Mâyâ, that Power of Her whereby what is impossible to us becomes possible. Mâyâ is Shakti but
Shakti is not to be identified only with this form of It. In the thirty-
six Tattvas, Mâyâ is a particular and comparatively gross form of
Shakti which appears after the evolution of the Sadvidyâ Tattva.
It is defined as that Shakti which is the sense of difference
(Bhedabuddhi) ; that is the power whereby the individual consciousness, distinguishing itself from others, considers itself separate from
them. Shakti is understood differently in the Shâkta Tantra and
in Shangkaras Mâyâvâda ; a matter of primary importance from
the point of view of Sâdhanâ and with which I will deal on some
future occasion. Whatever be the description given, all accounts
must end in the inconceivable Shakti (Achintyâ Shakti). She
the One, the primordial Shakti (Âdyâshakti) appears as many ; and
so the Shâkta Sâdhaka saying " Aham Devî nachânyosmi (I am
the Devî and none other) thinks to himself " Sâham " (I am
She).

NÂDA—THE FIRST PRODUCED MOVEMENT.

Shakti-tattva dealt with in the preceding article is really the
negative aspect of the Shiva-tattva. Though spoken of separately,
the two are indissolubly one. Shakti-tattva as the Tattva-sandoha
says is the Will of Shiva as yet unmanifest :—

Ichchhâ saiva svachchhâ santatasamavâyinî satî shaktih.

Sacharâcharasya jagato bîjam nikhilasya nijanilînasya.

These two Principles (Shiva-shakti Tattva) are the ultimate
Potency of creation, and as and when they (considered as one
Tattva) commence to act, the first movement towards manifestation
takes place. After the previous restful state of Shiva-Shakti there
follows the union for the purpose of creation of the two principles
which are Shivatattva and Shaktitattva. So it is said in the Shâkta
Tantra, " Shiva-Shakti-samâyogât jâyate srishtikalpanâ" (From the
union of Shiva and Shakti arises creative ideation). This union
and mutual relation is called Nâda. As the relation is not some
substantial thing apart from Shiva or Shakti, Nâda is really Shiva-
Shakti; passing from the state of mere potency into that of the first
ideating movement, from which at length, when finally perfected,
the whole universe is evolved. The Shâkta Tantras frequently
employ erotic symbolism to explain the creative process. This has

led a missionary author to the conclusion that "throughout its symbolism and pseudo-philosophisings there lies at the basis of the whole system... .....the conception of the sexual relationship as the ultimate explanation of the universe." An American author reviewing one of my works has called it "a doctrine for suffragette monists"—"religious feminism run mad." Both statements are examples of those depreciative misunderstandings which are so common in western descriptions of eastern belief and which seem so absurd to anyone who has understood the subject. How can "sexual relationship" which exists on the gross plane of matter be the ultimate explanation of That which has manifested not only this but all other relations and subjects. As for "feminism" and the supposed priority of the feminine principle, the doctrine has no more to do with either than with old age pensions or any other social question. We are not dealing with the biological question whether the female antedates the male principle, or the social question of the rights of Woman, but with those ultimate dual principles, aspects of the one active Consciousness, which projects from Itself both man and woman and all other dualities in the universe. Shiva and Shakti are one and neither is higher than the other. But how are European writers to be blamed when we find a distinguished Indian Sanskritist affirming that according to Shâkta doctrine "God *is* a woman" (the italics are mine).

Shakti is spoken of as female, that is, as Mother, because that is the aspect of the Supreme in which It is thought of as the Genetrix and Nourisher of the universe. But God is neither male nor female. As the Yâmala says for the benefit of all such ignorance "neyam yoshit na cha pumân na shandah na jadah smritah." These are all symbolisms borrowed from the only world which we ordinarily know—that around us. As for the charge of pseudo-philosophy, if it be that, then the same criticism must apply to the Advaitavâda Vedânta. For the Shâkta Tantra is the Sâdhanâ-shâstra of Advaitavâda presenting the teachings of Vedânta in its own manner and in terms of its own ritual symbolism. Thus it is said that Nâda is the Maithuna of Shiva and Shakti and that when Mahâkâla was in Viparîta Maithuna with Mahâkâlî (a form of Maithuna again which is symbolical of the fact that Shiva is Nishkriya and Shakti Sakriyâ)—there issued Bindu. For Maithuna others substitute the logical term Mithah'samavâyah as a description of Nâda which is Kriyâshakti. Before the appearance of Shabda there must be two. Unity is necessarily actionless. Two involves a third—which is the relation of both; a Trinity of Power which is reflected in the Trimûrti of the Mayik world as Brahmâ, Vishnu, Rudra.

From Nâda came Mahâbindu and this latter defferentiated into the Tribindu which is Kâmakalâ, the Mûla of all Mantras. In Pralaya, Shiva and Shakti exist as the "two in one"; Shiva as Chit, Shakti as Chidrûpinî; the Parâ Shakti—not being different or separated from Shiva (Avinâbhâvasambandha) and being undivided supreme Chit-Shakti (Akhandaparachichchhakti).

The Shâradâ-Tilaka (1-7) then says :—from the Sakalapara-meshvara vested with the wealth of Sachchidânanda (Sachchidâ-nandavibhavâl) appeared Shakti (Shakti Tattva); from Shakti, Nâdâ and from Nâda, Bindu (Mahâbindu). Sakala means with Kalâ ; that is the Brahman with what the Sângkhya calls Mûlaprakriti, that which the Vedânta calls Avidyâ and the Shâkta Tantras or Âgamas call Shakti. On the other hand Nishkala Shiva is Nirguna Shiva or that aspect of the Brahman which is unconnected with the creative Shakti ; just as Sakala Shiva is the Brahman so associated, Shiva in either aspect is always with Shakti; for Shakti is but Himself ; but whereas the Shakti associated with Paramashiva is Chidrûpinî and Vishovtûrnâ or beyond the Universe, the Shakti which is associated with the creative Shiva is that which appears as the Universe (Vishvâtmaka). The Parashakti is one with Chaitanya at rest. The other aspect which ripens into Nâda and Bindu denotes the "swollen" condition of readiness (Uchchhûnâ-vasthâ) of Her who existed in a subtle state in the great dissolution (Mahâpralaya). These two Shaktis (Nâda, Bindu) are stages in the movement towards the manifestation of the Self as object, that is as the Universe. In these the mere readiness or potency of Shaktitattva to act develops into action. In Nâdashakti therefore Kriyâ pre-dominates. When we speak of stages, development and so forth we are using language borrowed from the manifested world which in the sense there understood are not appropriate to a state prior to manifestation ; for such manifestation does not take place until after the appearance of the Purusha-Prakriti Tattva and the development from the latter of the impure Tattvas from Buddha to Prithivî. But a Sâdhanâ Shâstra, even if it had the power to do otherwise, could not usefully use terms and symbols other than those borrowed from the world of the Sâdhaka. The Prayogasâra says that the Shakti who is "turned towards" the state of liberation (Nirâmayapadonmukhî) awakes as Nâda and is turned to Shiva (Shivonmukhî) at which time She is said to be male (Pungrûpa). For then She becomes Hang in Hangsa. She who was one with Parashiva in Pralaya as the coalesced "I" (Aham) and " This "

2

(Idam) now in Her creative aspect as Shaktitattwa transforms Herself into Nâda. Nâda is action (Kriyâshakti rûpa). In simple language, potency and readiness to create, (Shaktitattva) becomes for the first time active as Nâda and then more so as Bindu which is a further development of Kriyâ Shakti dealt with in the next article.

According to Râghava Bhatta in his Commentary on the Shâradâ some writers do not speak of Nâda, though the author of the Shâradâ does so in order to indicate the sevenfold character of Târa. The Nâda state is however indicated by those Âchâryyas who speak of Kâla. So it is said "in the Kâlatattva which is Sound" (Ravâtmani kâlatattve). In the Hymn to Bhuvaneshî also it is said "Obeisance to Thee who art called Tattva in the character of Sound" (Namaste ravatvena tattvâbhidâne).

Nâda occupies the same place in the Mantra scheme as the Sadâkhya Tattva of the 36 Tattvas, for Bindu is Ishvara Tattva. As Consciousness reaches forth to enjoyment and the " I " is separated from the "This," what was mere diffusive consciousness as Sadâkhya Tattva is objectified into the all-embracing Âkâsha the Guna of which is gross Shabda ; that is something experienced as an objec' apparently different from and other than ourselves.

Nâda which etymologically means "Sound" is a technical term of the Mantrashâstra. The latter Shâstra is concerned with Mantravidyâ, and Mantra is manifested Shabda which also literally means "Sound." By "Sound" of course is not meant gross sound which is heard by the ear and which is the property of the Kâryyâkâsha developed as a Vikriti from the Prakriti Tattva which, with the Purusha Tattva, occupies the place (though without its dualities) of the Purusha and Prakriti of the Sângkhyas. Gross sound belongs to the impure creation as a Guna of Âkâsha or the ether which fills space. To avoid misconception, it is better to use the word Shabda which with Artha is manifested in the " Garland (or Rosary) of Letters" (Varnamâlâ) with which I will deal on some future occassion.

Nâda is the most subtle aspect of Shabda, as the first putting forth of Kriyâshakti. Paranâda and Parâvâk are Parâshakti. Nâda into which it evolves is the unmanifested (avyaktâtmâ) seed or essence (Nâdamâtrâ) of that which is later manifested as Shabda, devoid of particularities such as letters and the like (Varnâdivishesharahitah). It develops into Bindu which is of the same character. From the Mantra aspect as the source of Shabda this Mahâbindu as it differentiates to "create" is called the Shabdabrahman. Bindu when differentiated is also the source of the Vikritis or Tattvas and of their Lords (Tattvesha). In its character as Shabdabrahman it is the source of the manifested Shabda and Artha (Shabda-shabdârthakâranam). Shabdabrahman is thus a name of Brahman as the immediate creative source of the manifold Shabda and Artha.

What Shabdabrahman is, has been the subject of contention, as Râghava Bhatta's Commentary shows. It is sufficient to say here (where we are only concerned with Shabdabrahmâtmaka Bindu so far as it is necessary to explain Nâda) that Râghavabhatta rightly says that Shabdabrahman is the Chaitanya in all beings (Chaitanyam sarvvabhûtânam). This cosmic Shakti exists in the individual bodies of all breathing creatures (Prânî) in the form of Kundalini (Kundalîrûpâ). Nâda therefore which assumes the aspect of Bindu is also Chaitanya and Shakti. Nâda is thus the first emanative stage in the production of Mantra. The second is Bindu, or Shabdabrahman ; the third is Tribindu (Bindu, Nâda and Bîja) or Kâmakalâ ; the fourth is the production of Shabda as the Mâtrikâs which are the subtle state of the subsequently manifested gross letters (Varna) ; and the last is these gross letters, (Sthûlashabda) which compose the manifested Shabda or Mantra composed of letters (Varna) Syllables (Pada) and sentences (Vâkya). Thus Mantra ultimately derives from Nâda which is itself the Kriyâshaktirûpa aspect of Shiva-shakti who are the Supreme Nâda (Paranâda) and Supreme Speech (Parâvâk). The Prayogasâra says " Oh Devî that Antarâtmâ in the form of Nâda (Nâdâtmâ) itself makes sound (Nadate svayam) that is displays activity. Urged on by Vâyu (that is the Prânavâyu in Jîvas) it assumes the form of letters." Nâda again is itself divided into several stages, namely, Mahânâda or Nâdânta, the first movement forth of the Shabdabrahman ; Nâda when Shakti fills up the whole Universe with Nâdânta ; in other words the completed movement of which Nâdânta is the commencement ; and Nirodhinî which is that aspect of Nâda in which its universal operation having been completed, it operates in a particular manner and is transformed into Bindu, which is the completion of the first movement of Shakti, in which She assumes the character of the Creative Lord of the Universe (Ishvara Tattva). Nâdânta considered as the end and not the commencement of the series is that in which there is dissolution of Nâda (Nàdasya anta layah). Above Bindu, the Shaktis which have been already given in previous articles become more and more subtle until Nishkala Unmanî is reached which, as the Yoginîhridaya says, is uncreate motionless speech (Anutpan-nanishpandâvâk), the twin aspects of which are Samvit or the

Void (Sbûnya Samvit) and Samvit as tendency to manifestation in a subtle state (Utpatsuh samvid utpatyavasthâ sûkshmâ). Unmani is beyond Kâranarûpâ Shakti; where there is no experience (Bhânam) or Kala or Kalâ nor of Devatâ or Tattva, in the sense of category, as that which distinguishes one thing from another. It is Svanirvânamparam padam, the Nirvikalpaniranjanashivashakti which is Guruvaktra.

Nâda and Bindu exist in all Bîja Mantras which are generally written with the Bindu above and the Nâda below, for this is the form of the written Chandrabindu. In however some of the old pictorial representations of Ongkâra the real position of Nâda is shown as being over Bindu as an inverted crescent. Thus the great Bîja, Hrîm (ह्रीं) is composed of Ha, Ra, î and Ma. Of these Ha=Akâsha, Ra = Agnî, I = Ardhanârîshvara and M = Nâdabindu. The five Bhûtas are divided into two groups Amûrtta (formless) and Mûrtta (with form). Both Akâsha and Vâyu belong to the first group, because until the appearance of Agni as Rûpa, there is no colour and form. Agni therefore heads the second division. When Akâsha is with Agni there is form ; for Ra is the first manifestation of Rûpa. This form is in Ardhanârîshvara the combined Shiva-Shakti who hold all in themselves. The first three letters represent the Akâra or form aspect. The Mantra receives its complete form by the addition of the Mâhâtmya which is Nâda-bindu which are Nirâkâra (formless) and the Kârana (cause) of the other three in which they are implicitly and potentially contained ; being in technical phrase Antargata of, or held within, Bindu which again is Antargata of all the previously evolving Shaktis mentioned. The meaning of the Bîja Mantra then is that the Chidâkâsha is associated (Yukta) with Rûpa. It is thus the Shabda statement of the birth of General Form ; that is Form as such of which all particular forms are a derivation. Hrîm is, as pronounced, the gross-body as sound of the ideation of Form as such in the Cosmic Mind.

The degree of subtlety of the Shaktis preceding and following Nâda is in the Mantra Shâstra indicated by what is called "the utterance time" (Uchchâranakâla). Thus taking Bindu as the unit : Unmanî is Nirâkâra and Niruchchâra, formless and without utterance, undefined by any adjective : being beyond mind and speech and the universe (Vishvottîrhâ). The Uchchâranakâla of Samanî (so named Manahsahitatvât : on account of its association with mind ; the preceding Shakti Unmanî being tadrahitâ or devoid of that,) is 1/256, of Vyâpikâ 1/128 and so on to

Nâdânta 1/32, Nâda 1/16 to Ardhachandra which is 1/2 of Bindu and to Bindu itself.

Nâda is thus in Mantra Shâstra that aspect of Shakti which evolves into Bindu which later as differentiating into the Tribindu is called the Shabdabrahman who is the creative source of Shabda and Artha and thus of the revealed Shabda which Mantra is.

I would in conclusion meet an objection, which I have heard urged, namely that the Mantra Shâstra treats its subject with unnecessary complexity of detail. It is undoubtedly difficult and requires careful study. Simple minds may be satisfied with the statement that God created the world. Veda too gives an explanation of the cosmic problem in two words " He saw" (Sa aikshata). But who saw, and what, and how did He see? How also if there be only One came there to be anything to see? And what is to see (Îkshana). For the process is not like looking out of a window and seeing a man passing. " He " is Consciousness which is in Itself (Svarûpa) actionless. How then did " It " see and thus become active? Because It has two aspects one (Nishkalashiva) in which It is actionless and the other (Sakalashiva) in which it is Activity as the embodiment of all the Sangskâras. In this last aspect it is called Shakti. The latter term denotes Active Consciousness. How can one and the same thing have two contradictory aspects? We cannot say, otherwise than by affirming Svabhâva. By way of analogy we can refer to what psychology calls dual and multiple personalities. The ultimate Reality is alogical and unexplainable (Anirvachanîya). That it is one and not two is, it is said, proved by Veda and the actual experience (Svânubhava) had in Yoga. What is " seeing " ? It is not the observing of something outside which was there before it was observed. " Seeing" is the rising into consciousness (void of objects) of the memory of past universes existing in the form of the Sangskâras. Before this can occur, Consciousness must obscure to itself its nature and (though in truth an unity) must experience itself as an " I " observing a " This " which it has through Mâyâ Shakti projected outside Itself. There is no answer again to the question how this is possible except inscrutable Shakti (Achintyâ Shakti). But just as a man rising from deep sleep has first a more or less bare awareness which is gradually filled out with the thought of self and particular objects ; consciousness coming to itself, so that in the waking state it again recognises the world which had vanished utterly in dreamless slumber ; so it is with the Cosmic Consciousness. Just as man does not pass at once from dreamless slumber to the fullest waking perception ; so neither does

14

the Cosmic Consciousness. It passes gradually from its dreamless slumber (Sushupti) state which is the general dissolution (Mahāpralaya) to the waking state (Jāgrat) which is consciousness of the gross universe. The degrees in this emanative process are the Tattvas described in the last article. Manifestation, which is nothing but presentation of apparently external objects to the inner consciousness, is, as experienced by the limited consciousness, gradual. The seeds of the "I" and "This" are first formed and then grown. The first principal stage is that before and in Ishvara Tattva or Bindu and which therefore includes Nāda. The second is that of the world-consciousness arising through the agency of Māyā-shakti. These two stages are marked by two principal differences. In the first the "This" (Idam) is seen as part of the self, the two not being differentiated in the sense of inner and outer. In the second the object is externalised and seen as different from the self. In the first, when the Self experiences itself as object, the latter is held as a vague undefined generality. There is, as it were, an awareness of self-scission in which the self as subject knows itself as object and nothing more. The degrees in this process have been already explained. In the second not only is the object defined as something which appears to be not the self, but there are a multiplicity of objects each marked by its own differences ; for Māyā has intervened. The whole world-process is thus a re-awaking of the Cosmic Consciousness from sleep to the world, into which at Dissolution it had fallen ; and the Tattvas mark the gradual stages of re-awakening, that is re-awakening to the world, but a falling into sleep so far as true Consciousness is concerned. So in Kundalīyoga when Kundalinī sleeps in the Mūlādhāra man is awake to the world ; and when She awakes, the world vanishes from Consciousness which then regains its own state (Svarūpa). There is no reason to suppose that, judged in the terms of our present experience, the change is other than gradual. But how, it may be asked, is this known or what the stages are ; for were we there ? As individuals we were not ; for we speak of that which preceded the formation of the Sakala Jīva Consciousness. But Jīva was there as the plant is in the seed. It is the one Shiva who displays himself in all the Tattvas. Those who fall back into the seed have experience of it. There are, however, two bases on which these affirmations rest. In the first place there is correspondence between all planes. "What is without, is so manifested because it is within" ; not of course in the exact form in which it exists without but in the corresponding form of its own plane. We may therefore look for instruction to our daily life and its psychological states to discover both the elements and the working of the cosmic process. These also disclose a gradual unfolding of consciousness from something in the nature of mere awareness to the definite perception of a variety of multiple objects. But the normal experience is by its nature limited. That normal experience is, however, transcended in Yoga-states when consciousness becomes Nirâlambapurî, that is, detached from worldly objects : the experience wherein is (in part at least) available for the instruction of others. Secondly the Shâstras are records of truth beyond the senses (Atîndriya Tattva). •The Tattvas are not put forth as mere speculative guesses or imaginings of what might have been. When, however, supersensual truth is described in language it is necessarily expressed in terms, and with the use of symbols, of present experience. That experience is had under conditions of time and space and others. We know and speak of mere potency ripening into actuality, of potential energy becoming more and more kinetic, of shifting states of consciousness, and so forth. These are matters the knowledge of which is drawn from the world around us. But this does not necessarily make them wholly untrue or unreal as applied to higher planes. One of the commonest errors is to raise false partitions between things. The experience is real for it is Shiva's and His experience is never unreal. It is according to its degree (that is on its plane) real ; an expression (limited though it be) of the ultimate Reality Itself. We can think in no other terms. But it is also true that these terms and symbols, having only complete validity on our plane, are no longer wholly true for Consciousness as it rises from it. But other forms of Consciousness must take their place until the Formless is reached. The Tattvas explain (limited though such explanation be by the bounds of our thought and language) the modes through which the returning Consciousness passes until it rests in Itself (Svarûpavishrânti) and has Peace. And so the Buddhist Mantrayâna aptly defines Yoga in the sense of result, (which in Tibetan is called rNal-rByor) as the " Finding rest or peace". This final state, as also those intermediate ones which lie between it and the normal individual world-consciousness, are only actually realised in Jnâna Yoga (by whatsoever method Jnâna is attained) when the mind has been wholly withdrawn from without and faces the operative power of Consciousness behind it (Nirâmayapadonmukhî).

But here we are dealing with Mantrayoga when the mind is thinking the states which Jnâna, in whatever degree, realises as Consciousness. The Mantra Shâstra looks at the matter, of which we write, from the standpoint of Mantra that is of manifested Shabda its object. Kundalinî is both Jyotirmayî, Her Sûkshma-

16

rûpâ ; and Mantramayî Her Sthûlarûpa. We begin with the latter.
All things are then defined in terms of Shabdârtha and of the
various causal forms which precede it. The first of such produced
forms is Nâda which becomes Bindu and then on the differentiation
of the Tattvas the "hidden sound" (Avyaktarava), the Logos or
Cosmic Word utters " the Garland of Letters " (Varnamâlâ) of which
all Mantras are formed. It traces the degrees in which the idealing
Cosmic Consciousness becomes, as Supreme Speech (Parâvâk), the
Genetrix of the subtle and gross Shabda which are the Mâtrikâs
and Varnas respectively. That Supreme Speech (Parâvâk) is without idea or language, but is represented as gradually assuming the
state in which it utters both and projects from Itself into the sensual
world the objects (Artha) which they denote. The actual manifestation of these from Parashabda through Pashyantî, Madhyamâ
and Vaikharî, will be described in another article.

The practice of Mantra Yoga not only gives, from a merely
intellectual standpoint, an understanding of Vedânta which
cannot ordinarily be had by the mere reading of philosophical
texts ; but also produces a pure Bhâva ripening into Mahâbhâva
through the purification of mind (Chittashuddhi) which such
practice (according to the rules of Sâdhanâ laid down in
the Tantras or Mantrashâstra) gives, as one of its Siddhis.
What the Western, and sometimes the English educated
Indian, does not understand or recognise, is the fact that
the mere reading of Vedantic texts without Chittashuddhi will
neither bring true understanding or other fruitful result. The
experienced will find that this apparent complexity and wealth of
detail is not useless and is, from an extra-ritual standpoint, to a
considerable extent, and from that of Sâdhanâ wholly, necessary.
A friend of mine was once asked by a man in a somewhat testy
manner " to give him a plain exposition of the Vedânta in five
minutes." It takes years to understand perfectly any science or
profession. How can that, which claims to explain all, be
mastered in a short talk ? But more than this ; however prolonged
the intellectual study may be, it must, to be really fruitful, be
accompanied by some form of Sâdhanâ. The Tantra Shâstra
contain this for the Hindu, though it is open to him or any other
to devise a better if he can. Forms ever change with the ages,
while the Truth which they express, remains.

BINDU OR BHAKTI READY TO CREATE.

From Nâda, previously described, evolved Bindu (Nâda-bindu-samudbhavah). What then is Bindu ? Literally the term means a " drop" or a " point " such as the Anusvâra breathing. But in the Mantra Shâstra it has a technical meaning. It is not, as a distinguished Indian Sanskritist called it merely a " drop." It is not that " red drops" mix with " white drops " and so forth a description of his which reminds one more of the pharmacy or sweet shop than the Shâstra. This and other statements betray an ignorance of Indian tradition and a mental attitude alien to Indian thinking which distinguishes so many of those whose souls have been captured in the net of an English education. Those who speak another's language and think another's thought must see to it that their own Indian self is not, through the dangers to which it is thus exposed, lost. But even an educated Western, ignorant of the Shâstra, but with a knowledge of the history of religious thought would have perceived the significance of the term Bindu when he had learnt that one of its literal meanings was a " Point.'

In an anonymous Mystical Work published in the eighteenth century by one of the " French Protestants of the Desert" called Le Mystêre de la Croix, it is said (p. 9). " Ante omnia Punctum exstitit ; non to atomon, aut mathematicum sed diffusivum. Monas erat explicite : implicite Myrias. Lux erat, erant et Tenebrae ; Principium et Finis Principii. Omnia et nihil : Est et non."

" Before all things were, there was a Point (Punctum : Bindu) not the Atom or mathematical point (which though it is without magnitude has position) but the diffusive (neither with magnitude nor position). In the One (Monas) there was implicitly contained the Many (Myrias). There was Light and Darkness : Beginning and End : Everything and Nothing : Being and Non-being (that is, the state was neither Sat nor Asat)." The author says that the all is engendered from the central indivisible Point of the double triangle (that is what is called in the Tantras Shatkona Yantra) regarded as the symbol of creation. " Le Tout est engendré du point central indivisible du double triangle." This " Point" is one of the world's religious symbols and is set in the centre of a Shat-kona as above or in a circular Mandala or sphere. On this symbol St. Clement of Alexandria in the second century A.D. says that if abstraction be made from a body of its properties, its depth, breadth, and then length " the point which remains is a unit, so to speak, having position ; from which if we abstract position there is the notion of unity" (Stromata V.12. Ante Nicene Library Vol.

IV). Again Shelley in his "Prometheus" says "plunge into eternity where recorded time seems but a point."

Where does the universe go at the Great Dissolution (Mahā-pralaya)? It collapses so to speak into a Point. This point may be regarded as a mathematical point in so far as it is without any magnitude whatever but as distinguished from it, in that it has in fact no position. For there is then no notion of space. It need hardly be said that this is a symbol, and a symbol borrowed from our present experience cannot adequately represent any state beyond it. We only conceive of it as a point as something infinitesimally subtle which is in contrast with the extended manifested universe which is withdrawn into it. This Point is Bindu. But this again is to make use of material images borrowed from the world of objective form. Bindu is an aspect of Shakti or Consciousness; therefore it is interpreted also in terms of our present consciousness. As so interpreted and as Îshvara Tattva, which it is, Shakti is called Bindu ; because here consciousness completely identifies itself with the universe as unmanifested Idam and thus subjectifies it and becomes with it a point of consciousness. Thus by way of example the individual mind is completely subjectified and exists for each of us as a mathematical point (and so it is spoken of by some as being of atomic dimension) though the body to the extent to which it is not subjectified appears as an object or extended thing. We never conceive of our own minds as extended because of this complete subjectification. In the same way the consciousness of Îshvara completely subjectifies the universe. He does not of course see the universe as a multiplicity of objects outside and different from Himself : for if He did He would be Jivâ and not Îshvara. He sees it as an object which is a whole and which whole is Himself. In Sadâkhya Tattva "Otherness" (Idam) is presented to Consciousness by Shakti. This Idam is then faintly perceived (to use the language of the Vimarshinî on Îshvara-Pratyabhijnâ III. 1, 2) "in a hazy fashion (Dhyâmala-prâyam) "like a picture just forming itself" (Unmîlita-mâtra-chitra-kalpam) ; seen by the mind only and not as something seen without by the senses (Antah-karanaika-vedyam). The object thus vaguely surges up into the field of consciousness in which the emphasis is on the cognitive aspect or "I" (Aham). This however is not the "I" or "this" of our experience, for it is had in the realms beyond Mâyâ. The "This" is then experienced as part of the Self. In Îshvara Tattva all haziness gives place to clarity of the "This," which is thus seen completely as part of the Self ; the emphasis being on the "This." After equal emphasis on the "I" and "This" in Shuddhavidyâ Tattva the two are wholly separated by Mâyâ. When therefore the Yogî passes beyond the Mâyik world his first higher experience is in this Tattva.

Nâda and Bindu are states of Shakti in which the germ of action (Kriyâ-shakti) so to speak increasingly sprouts with a view to manifestation producing a state of compactness of energy and readiness to create. Râghava Bhatta (Comm. Shâradâ I. 7) speaks of them as two states of Shakti which are the proper conditions (Upayogyâvasthâ) for creation. They are like all else aspects of Shakti, but are names of those aspects which are prone to and ready for creation (Uchchhûnâvasthâ). Bindu is said to be the massive or Ghanâvastha state of Shakti. The Prapanchasâra Tantra says that Shakti is seized with the desire to create and becomes Ghanîbhûtâ (Vichikîrshu ghanîbhûtâ). Thus milk becomes Ghanîbhûta when it turns into cream or curd. In other words Shakti is conceived as passing gradually from its subtle state through Shakti-tattva and Nâda (in its three stages) and becomes what is relatively gross or massive as Power which is fully equipped to pass from the stage of potency into that of active manifestation. That stage is Bindu which is called Mahâbindu or Parabindu to distinguish it from the other Bindus into which it subsequently differentiates.

The commentary of Kâlîcharana on the Shatchakranirûpana (see my Tantrik Texts, Vol. 2, V. 4) citing Todala Tantra (Ch. VI) says that the Supreme Light is formless; but Bindu implies both the Void (Shûnya) and Guna also. Bindu is the Void in so far as it is the Supreme Brahman. It implies Guna as being the creative or Shakti aspect of the Brahman which subsequently evolves into the Purusha and Prakriti Tattvas of which the latter is with Guna. The commentary to V. 49 states that this Bindu is the Lord (Ishvara) whom some Paurânikas call Mahâvishnu and others the Brahmapurusha? and (V. 37) that Parabindu is the state of "Ma" before manifestation; being Shiva-Shakti enveloped by Mâyâ. As to this it may be observed that the letter M is male, and Bindu which is the nasal breathing sounded as M is the unmanifested Shiva-Shakti or Ma which is revealed upon its subsequent differentiation into the three Shaktis from which the universe proceeds. Bindu as the cause is Chidgharâ or massive consciousness and Power in which lie potentially in a mass (Ghana), though undistinguishable the one from the other, all the worlds and beings about to be created. This is Parama-Shiva and in Him are all the Devatâs. It is thus this Bindu which is worshipped in secret by all Devas (V. 41) and which is indicated in its different phases in the Chandrabindu (Nada, Bindu) Shakti and Sirota of the Om and other Bija mantras.

This Bindu is in Satyaloka which, within the human body, exists in the pericarp of the thousand-petalled Lotus (Sahasrara) in the highest cerebral centre. It is, as I have already said, compared to a grain of gram (Chanaka) which under its outer sheath (which is Māyā) contains the two seeds (Shiva and Shakti) in close and undivided union.

Kālicharana (V. 40) thus cites the following : " In the Satyaloka is the formless and lustrous one. She is like a grain of gram devoid of hands, feet and the like. She has surrounded Herself by Māyā (that is She is about to create by the agency of this Power of Hers). She is Sun, Fire and Moon. She being intent on creation (Unmukhî) becomes twofold (Dvidhā bhitvā) and then, by differentiation of Shiva and Shakti, arises creative ideation (Srishtikalpanâ). Shiva and Shakti are of course not actually divided for they are not like a chupatti or some other material thing. It might seem unnecessary to make such obvious remarks did not experience tell me of the absurd misunderstandings which exist of the Scripture. When we read that God "is a woman," that the Shâkta Tantra is " Feminism " with a doctrine similar to that of Prof. Lester Ward's primacy of the female sex that " the conception of the sexual relationship is the ultimate explanation of the universe" and so forth, no caveats, however obvious, are unnecessary. What of course is meant is that whereas in Pralaya, Shiva and Shakti existed as one unity of consciousness, They in creation, whilst still remaining in themselves what they always were, project the universe which is Shakti ; and then we have the Paramâtmâ and Jîvâtmâ consciousness which seem to the latter to be different.

Although Parabindu and all which evolves from It are nothing but aspects of Shakti and in no wise different from It, yet as representing that state of Shakti which immediately precedes creation, it is this state of Shakti which is said to be the cause of the universe of name and form (Nâmarûpa) ; concepts and concepts objectified ; or Shabda the word and Artha its meaning. The states of Shakti preceding Bindu are those in which the Bindu state is in process of being " evolved " according to what we may call an Avikrita Parinâma and when evolved it is the cause of the universe. Really they are merely aspects of one and the same pure Shakti. This is not an evolution in time. As Plotinus says, the universe " was formed according to intellect (here the Cosmic

Power or Prapancha Shakti which manifests as Mahat) and intellect not preceding in time but prior " (in the sense that cause precedes effect). This again, as all descriptions, (in so far as they are applicable to the transcendent Shakti) is imperfect .for sequence of cause and effect involves to our minds the notion of time. This Supreme Bindu as containing in · Himself all Devatàs is the ultimate object of adoration by all classes of worshippers (V. 44) under the name of Shiva, or Mahâvishnu or the Devî as those call It "who are filled with a passion for Her Lotus Feet." The sectarianism of the lower mind, still existent in both East and West, is here shown to be a matter of words (the fight for which is of such interest to many) and is reduced to its real common denominator. As the Lord says in the Gîtâ, whomever men may worship all such worship comes eventually to Him.

Parabindu is thus the Head of every line of creation ; of the Tattvas or Vikritis from Buddhi to Prithivî and their Lords (Tattvesha) and of the Shabda or Mantra creation ; all belonging to the Vikàra Srishti or Parinâma Srishti. The development after the manifestation of Prakriti is a real evolution (Parinâma) for Consciousness has then been divided into subject and object in time and space. What is spoken of in terms of a development in the Ishvara body is not that. There Shakti assumes various aspects with a view to create but without manifestation. Shaktitattva, whilst remaining such, assumes the aspects of Nàda and Bindu.

The next stage is thus described in the Shâradâ Tilaka (Ch. I) as follows :—

Parashaktimayah sâkshât tridhâsau bhidyate punah
Bindur nâdo bîjamiti tasya bhedâh samîritâh
Binduh shivâtmako bîjang shaktir nâdastayor mithah
Samavâyah samâkhyâtah sarvâgamavishâradaih.

(That which is supreme Shakti again divides Itself into three, such divisions being known as Bindu, Nâda, Bîja. Bindu is said to be of the nature of Shiva and Bîja of Shakti, and Nâda is the mutual relation between these two, by those who are learned in the Āgamas).

One Ms. I have seen has Bindur nâdâtmako, but the commentary of the Shatchakra (V. 40) explains this as Shivâtmaka. These form the three Bindus (Tribindu). Nàda here again is Trait d'Union, the Yoga of the other two Bindus as the Prayogasàra calls it. (See Râghava's Comm. to V. 8 of Ch. 1 Shâradâ).

'These are Shiva, Shiva-Shakti, Shakti. By this it is not to be understood that Shiva or Shakti are ever altogether dissociated but the aspects may be regarded as Shiva or Shakti pradhâna respectively. Bhâskararâya in his valuable commentary on the Lalitâ Sahasranâma says "From the causal (Kârana) Bindu proceeds the effect (Kâryya) Bindu, Nâda and Bîja. Thus these three which are known as supreme, subtle and gross arose." (Asmâchcha kâranabindossâkshâttkramena kâryyabindustato nâdastato bîjam iti trayam utpannam tadidang parasûkshmasthûla-padairapyuchyate, V'132). .

One text of the Prapanchasâra Tantra says that the Parabindu divides into two parts, of which the right is Bindu, the Male Purusha or Hang, and the left Visarga the Female Prakriti or Sah making the combined Hangsah. Hangsah is the union of Prakriti and Purusha and the universe is Hangsah. In however the Ms. on which my edition of that Tantra is based (Tantrik Texts, Vol. III) it is said that the Bindu (Para) divided by Kâla becomes threefold as Bindu, Nâda, Bîja. Substantially the matter seems one of nomenclature for the two Bindus which make Visarga become three by the addition of the Shiva Bindu. Moreover as Hang is Shiva and Sah is Shakti, the combined Hangsah implies the relation which in the Shâradâ account is called Nâda. So it is also said from the first vowel issued "Hrîm," from the second Hangsah, and from the third the Mantra "Hrîm, Shrîm, Klîm," the first indicative of general form ; the second being a more Sthûla form of Âkâsha and Agni (Sha = Âkâsha ; Ra = Agni) held as it were within the "skin" (Charma) of the enveloping Ardhanârîshvara : the third commencing with the first and last letters including all the 24 Tattvas and all the fifty letters into which the general Form particularises itself.

Parabindu is Shiva-Shakti considered as undivided, undifferentiated principles. On the "bursting" of the seed which is the Parabindu the latter assumes a threefold aspect as Shiva or Bindu, Shakti or Bîja and Nâda the Shiva-Shakti aspect which, considered as the result, is the combination, and from the point of view of cause, the inter-relation of the two (Shâradâ V. 9) the one acting as excitant (Kshobhaka) and the other being the excited (Kshobhya). The commentary on V. 40 of the Shatchakranirûpana speaks of Nâda as the union of Shiva and Shakti ; as the connection between the two and as being in the nature of the Shakti of action (Kriyâshaktisvarûpâ). It is also said to be that the substance of which is Kundalî (Kundalinîmaya). All three are but different phases of Shakti in creation (Comm. V. 39) being different aspects of Parabindu which is itself the Ghanâvasthâ aspect of Shakti.

Thus in the first division of Shakti, Nâda, Bindu, Nâda is the Maithuna or Yoga of Shiva and Shakti to produce the Parabindu which again differentiates into threefold aspects as the Shaktis, though in grosser form, which produced it. Though the Gunas are factors of the gross Shakti Prakriti, they are in subtle form contained within the higher Shaktis. This Shakti as the first potentially kinetic aspect about to display itself is the Chit aspect of Shakti and Chit Shakti is, when seen from the lower level of the Gunas, Sâttvik ; Nâda is in the same sense Râjasik, for Shakti becomes more kinetic gathering together its powers, as it were from the previous state of barely stirring potency, for the state of complete readiness to create which is Bindu and which in the aforesaid sense as Ghanîbhûta foreshadows that Tamas Guna which at a lower stage is the chief factor which creates the world, for the latter is largely the product of Tamas. Each aspect of the Tribindu again is associated with one or other of the Gunas. These divisions of aspect from the Guna stand point are not to be understood as though they were separate and exclusively concerned with only one of the Gunas. The Gunas themselves never exist separately. Where there is Sattva there is also Rajas and Tamas. In the same way in the case of the three Shaktis Ichchhâ, Jnâna, Kriyâ from which the Gunas develop, one never stands by itself, though it may be predominant. Where there is Ichchhâ there is Jnâna and so forth. And so again Shakti, Nâda and Bindu are not to be severed like different objects in the Mayik world. In each there is implicitly or explicitly contained the other. Parameshvara assumes (for the Jîva) successively the triple aspects of Shakti, Nâda, Bindu, Kâryya Bindu, Bîja, Nâda, thus completing by this differentiation of Shakti the sevenfold causal sound-forms of the Pranava or Ongkâra ; namely Sakala Parameshvara (which is Sachchhidânanda for even when the Brahman is associated with Avidyâ its own true nature (Svarûpa) is not affected) Shakti (Shaktitattva) Nâda (Sadâkhya Tattva) Parabindu (Ishvara Tattva) Bindu (Kâryya) Nâda and Bîja. It is not clear to me where (if at all) the Shuddhavidyâ Tattva comes in according to this scheme, unless it be involved in Nâda the Mithah samavâya ; but the Purusha-Prakriti Tattvas appear to take birth on the division of the Parabindu into Shiva and Shakti or Hang and Sah ; Hangsah being the Purusha-Prakriti Mantra.

The first impulse to creation comes from the ripening of the Adrishta of Jîvas on which Sakala Parameshvara puts forth His

Shakti (which means Himself as Shakti) to produce the Universe wherein the fruits of Karma may be suffered and enjoyed. All the above seven states are included in, and, constitute, the first stage of Ikshana or "Seeing" and is that state in which Shabda exists in its supreme or Para form (Parashabdasrishti). She who is eternal (Anādirūpā) existing subtly as Chidrūpinī in Mahāpralaya becomes on the ripening of Adrishta inclined (Utsuka) for the life of form and enjoyment, and reveals Herself on the disturbance of the equilibrium of the Gunas. As the Vāyavīya Samhitā says "Parā Shakti through the will of Shiva is revealed with Shiva Tattva (for the purpose of creation). Then She manifests as the oil which is latent in, exudes from, the sesamum seed." Parameshvara is Saguna Shiva or the Īshvara of Vedānta Philosophy with Māyā as His Upādhi. He is Sat, Chit, Ānanda in Māyā body and endowed with all Shaktis (Sarvavedāntasiddhantasārasangraha 312, 313, 315). There is, as the Panchadashî says, (3-38), a Shakti of Shiva which is in and controls all things which have their origin in Ananda or Īshvara. When Īshvara is moved to create, this Īshvara-shakti or Māyā which is the aggregate of, and which yet transcends, all individual Shaktis issues from Him and from this Māyā issue all the particular Shaktis by which the universe is evolved and is maintained. The same substance is, to a large extent, to be found in all accounts under a variety of presentment or symbols; even where there are real differences due to the diversity of doctrine of different Vedantic schools. This is not the case here: for the account given is a Sādhanā presentment of Advaitavāda. The Shākta Tantra teaches the unity of Paramātmā and Jiva though its presentation of some subjects as Shakti, Māyā, Chidābhāsa is different (owing to its practical view point) from Shangkara's Māyāvāda. On this matter I may refer my readers to the article which I recently wrote on Shakti and Māyā in the second number of the *Indian Philosophical Review* (Baroda).

The three Bindus constitute the great Triangle of World-Desire which is the Kāmakalā; an intricate subject which I must leave for a future issue. The three Bindus are Sun, Moon and Fire and the three Shaktis Ichchhā, Jnāna, Kriyā associated with the three Gunas, Sattva, Rajas, Tamas. I do not here deal with the order or correspondence which requires discussion. From them issued the Devis Raudrī, Jyeshthā, Vāmā and from them the Trimūrti Rudra, Brahmā, Vishnu.

The three Bindus are also known as the white Bindu (Sitabindu), the red Bindu (Shonabindu) and the mixed Bindu

(Mishrabindu). These represent the Prakāsha, Vimarsha and Prakāsha-Vimarsha aspects of the Brahman which are called in the ritual Charanatritaya (The Three Feet). The Gurupādukā Mantra in which initiation is given in the last or Shadāmnāya Dīkshā represents a state beyond the Shukla, Rakta and Mishra Charanas. So it is said in Shruti that there are four Brahmapada, three here and one the Supreme which is beyond.

As is the case in many other systems the One for the purpose of creation is presented in twofold aspect for , Unity is actionless and their relation involves a third aspect which makes the Trinity. But this apparent differentiation does not derogate from the substantial unity of the Brahman. As the ancient Rudrayāmala (II. 22) says : "The three Devas Brahmā, Vishnu, Maheshvara are but one and formed out of My body."

Ekā mūrtistrayo devā brahmavishnumaheshvarāh
Mama vigrahasangkliptāh srijatyavati hanti cha.

From the differentiating Bindu are evolved the Tattvas from Buddhi to Prithivi and the six Lords of the Tattvas (preceding from Parashiva the seventh) who are the presiding Devatās of mind and of the five forms of matter. Here on the diremption or dichotomy of Consciousness, Mind and matter are produced. That is Consciousness functions in and through the self-created limitations of mind and matter. It was on this division also that there arose the Cosmic Sound (Shabda Brahman) which manifests as Shabda and Artha. This is the Shabda-brahman ; so called by those who know the Āgamas.

Bhidyamānāt parādvindor avyaktātmā ravo' bhavat,
Shabdabrahmeti tang prāhuh sarvāgamavishāradāh.

(Shārada Tilaka I-11).

It will be observed that in this verse the first Bindu is called Para and to make this clear the author of the Prānatoshini adds the following note: " By Parabindu is meant the first Bindu which is a state of Shakti (Parādvindoarityanena shaktyavasthārūpo yah prathamabindustasmāt). Shabda-brahman is the Brahman in its aspect as the immediate undifferentiated Cause of the manifested and differentiated Shabda or language in prose or verse ; and of Artha or the subtle or gross objects which thought and language denote. It is thus the causal state of the manifested Shabda or Mantra.

PRINTED BY THOMPSON AND CO., AT THE "MINERVA PRESS,"
83, POPHAM'S BROADWAY, MADRAS.

. STUDIES 2172

IN

MANTRA SHÂSTRA

PART III

(Maya Tattva, The Kanchukas, Hangsa)

BY

ARTHUR AVALON

July 1915

(Reprinted from the "Vedanta Kesari")

PRINTED BY
THOMPSON AND CO., AT THE "MINERVA" PRESS.
83, POPHAM'S BROADWAY. MADRAS.

STUDIES IN THE MANTRA SHÂSTRA,

(MÂYÂ TATTVA).

BY

ARTHUR AVALON.

What Matter is in itself the senses do not tell us. All that can be predicated of it is its effect upon these senses. The experiencer is affected in five different ways giving rise in him to the sensations of hearing (Shabda); feel by which is experienced the thermal quality of things (Sparsha); colour and form (Rûpa); taste (Rasa); and smell (Gandha). The cause of these are the five Bhûtas which, in the general cosmic evolution, are derived from the Tanmâtra or general elements of the particulars of sense perception. These again together with the senses (Indriya) or faculties of mind operating through a particular physical organ as their instrument and Manas the mental faculty of attention, selection and synthesis of the discrete manifold, derive from the still more general aspects of the Cosmic Mind or Antahkarana which are the personal and impersonal forms of limited experience respectively called Ahangkâra and Buddhi. These again are evolutes from that form of Shakti which is Prakriti Tattva and which in the 36 Tattva scheme comes into being through the instrumentality of Mâyâ Shakti from the preceding Tattvas of the pure creation extending from Shuddhavidyâ to Shivashakti-Tattva; the Svarûpa of the last being Sachchidânanda or Pure Spirit. Matter is thus a manifestation or aspect of Spirit. The two are ultimately one. They seem to be two because the fundamental Feeling (Chit) is able as Shakti to experience itself as object. As Professor Haeckel says, in conformity with Shâkta Monism, Spirit and matter are not two distinct entities but two forms or aspects of one single fundamental Substance (which is here the Brahman). The one entity with dual aspect is the sole Reality which presents itself to view as the infinitely varied picture of the universe. The two are inseparably combined in every atom which, itself and its forces, possess the elements not only of vitality but of further development in all degrees of consciousness and will. The ultimate substance is Shakti which is of dual aspect as Chit-Shakti which represents the spiritual and Mâyâ-Shakti which represents the material aspect. These are not separable. In the universe the former is the Spirit-matter and the latter Matter-spirit. The two exist in inseparable connection (Avinabhâva Sambandha) as inseparable (to use a simile of the Shaiva Shâstra) as the winds of the heaven from the ether in which they blow. Manifested Shakti or Mâvâ is the universe. Unmanifest Shakti is feeling consciousness (Chidrûpâ). Mâyâ-Shakti appears as subtle mind and as gross matter and as the life-force and is in Herself (Svarûpa) consciousness. There is and can be nothing absolutely lifeless or unconscious because Shakti is in itself Being—Feeling—Consciousness—Bliss(Chidrûpinî, ânandamayî) beyond all worlds (Vishvottîrnâ); and appears as apparently unconscious or partly conscious and partly unconscious material forms in the universe (Vishvâtmaka). The universe is Shakti. Therefore it is commingled Spirit-matter. Shakti beyond all worlds is Consciousness. The one Consciousness exists throughout ; when changeless it receives the name of Shiva ; when the source of and as all moving objects it is called Shakti.

The universe arises through a negation or Veiling of true Consciousness. As the Spandakârika says "By veiling the own true form its Shaktis ever arise" (Svarûpâvarane châsya shaktayah sattatotthitâ). This is a common doctrine of the three schools here discussed. The difference lies in this that in Sângkhya it is a second independent principle (Prakriti) which veils ; in Mâyâvâda Vedânta it is the non-brahman unexplainable mystery (Mâyâ) which veils, and in Shâkta Advaitavâda it is Consciousness which, without ceasing to be such, yet veils itself. This statement shortly describes the difference in the three concepts which may however be more fully elaborated.

The Mahânirvâna Tantra says that the Vâkya " All is verily Brahman" (Sarvam khalvidam Brahma) is the basis of Kulâchâra. But Brahman is Consciousness ; and it cannot be denied that there is an element of apparent unconsciousness in things. Sângkhya says that this is due to another Principle independent of the Purusha-consciousness namely the unconscious Prakriti, which is real notwithstanding its changes. But according to Advaitavâda Vedânta there is only one Reality. It therefore denies the existence of any second independent principle. Shangkara attributes unconsciousness to the unexplainable (Anirvachanîya) Wonder Mâyâ, which is neither real (Sat) nor unreal (Asat) nor partly real and partly unreal (Sadasat) and which though not forming part of Brahman, and therefore not Brahman, is yet, though not a second reality, unseparately associated and sheltering with Brahman

(Máyâbrahmâshritâ) in one of its aspects (Ishvara) ; owing what false appearance of reality it has to the Brahman with which it is so associated. . It is an eternal falsity (Mithyabhūtasanâtanî) unthinkable, alogical, unexplainable (Anirvachanîya). The reflection of Purusha on Prakriti gives the appearence of consciousness to the latter. So also the reflection (Chidâbhâsa) of Brahman on unconscious Mâyâ is Ishvara and on unconscious Avidyâ is Jîva. Though Mâyâ is thus not a second reality the fact of positing it at all gives to Shangkara's doctrine a tinge of dualism from which the Shâkta doctrine (which has yet a weakness of its own) is free. The Shâkta doctrine has no need of Chidâbhâsa. It says that Mâyâ is a Shakti of Brahman and being Shakti, which is not different from the possessor of Shakti (Shaktimân), it is in its Svarûpa consciousness. It is then consciousness which veils itself ; not unconscious Mâyâ which veils consciousness. According to Shangkara man is the Spirit (Âtmâ) vestured in the Mâyik falsities of mind and matter. He accordingly can only establish the unity of Jîva and Ishvara by eliminating from the first Avidyâ and from the second Mâyâ, both being essentially—and from the transcendent standpoint, nothing. Brahman is thus left as common denominator. The Shâkta has need to eliminate nothing; Man's spirit or Âtmâ is Shiva. His mind and body are Shakti. Shiva and Shakti are one. The Jîvâtmâ is Shiva-Shakti, the latter being understood as in its world-aspect. So is the Paramâtmâ ; though here Shakti, being uncreating, is in the form of Consciousness (Chidrûpinî). The supreme Shiva-Shakti exists as one. Shiva-Shakti as the world is the Manifold. Man is thus not the Spirit covered by a non-brahman falsity but Spirit covering itself with its own Power or Shakti. As the Kaulâchâryya Sadânanda says in his Commentary (which I am about to publish) on the 4th Mantra of the Isha Upanishad—"The changeless Brahman which is consciousness appears in creation as Mâyâ which is Brahman (Brahmamayî) consciousness (Chidrûpinî) holding in Herself unbeginning (Anâdi) Karmik tendencies (Karmasangskâra) in the form of the three Gunas. Hence She is Gunamayî (Her substance is Guna) despite being Chinmayî (Consciousness). As there is no second principle these Gunas are Chit-Shakti." Hence, in the words of the Yoginîhridaya Tantra, the Devî is Prakâshavimarsha- sâmarasvarûpinî. There is thus truly no unconscious Mâyâ and no Chidabhâsa. All which exists is Consciousness as Shakti "Aham strî" as the Advaitabhâva Upanishad exclaims. And so the grand doctrine "All is consciousness" is boldly and vigorously affirmed. Those who worship the Mother worship nothing unconscious but a Supreme Consciousness which is Love, the body of which love is all forms of consciousness-unconsciousness produced by, and which is, Her as Shiva's Power. In short Shangkara says that there is unconsciousness which appears to be conscious through Chidâbhâsa. Shâkta doctrine says consciousness appears to be unconsciousness or more truly to have an element of unconsciousness in it (for nothing even empirically is absolutely unconscious) owing to the veiling play of consciousness itself as Mâyâ-Shakti. The result is in the end the same. "All is consciousness"—but the method by which this conclusion is attained and the presentment of the matter is reversed.

This presentment again is in conformity with scientific research which has shown that even so called "brute matter" exhibits the elements of that sentiency which, when evolved in man, is the full self-consciousness. It has been well said that sentiency is an integrant constituent of all existence physical as well as metaphysical and its manifestation can be traced throughout the mineral and chemical as well as the vegetable and animal worlds. It essentially comprises the functions of relation to environment, response to stimuli and atomic memory in the lower or inorganic plane whilst in the higher or organic plane it includes all the psychic functions such as consciousness, perception, thought, reason, volition and individual memory. Throughout it is the one Mother who works now veiling Her Bliss in inorganic matter, now more fully revealing Herself by gradual stages as the vitivity (which She is) displays itself in the evolving forms of worldly life. As Haeckel says, sentiency is like movement found in all matter. To reach this conclusion we must assume (as the Shaiva-Shâkta schools do) that Kriyâ with Ichchhâ, its preliminary, are functions of consciousness. Abhinava Gupta in his Commentary on the Pratyabhijnâ Kârikâ says "The characteristic of action is the manifestation of all objects. These objects again characterised by conciousness-unconsciousness are in the nature of a shining forth (A'bhâsa)." The universe is thus described as a "going forth" (Prasara) of Shiva.

The ultimate reality is Sachchidânanda which, as the source of appearances, is called Shakti. The latter in its Sat (Being) aspect is omnipresent-indestructible (eternal) Source and Basis both of the Cosmic Breath or Prâna as also of all vital phenomena displayed as the individual Prâna in separate and concrete bodies. Shakti is Life which, in its phenomenal sense as manifested in individual bodies, issues from and rests upon and at basis is Sat. In this aspect manifested Shakti is vitality which is the one fixed unalterable potential in the universe of which all other forms of energy are particular effects. Life is the phenomenal aspect of Spirit in which, as its cause, it is on the great dissolution merged. There is no absolute end to life but only to certain structures of life. As it had no end it has no absolute beginning. It appears only in creation from the depths of Being which is its unmanifested ground. The search for the "origin of life" is futile; for it had no origin but in Brahman who, in a supreme sense, is Infinite Life. Life is throughout the universe. Every atom of dust is quivering with it, as are the most sensitive organic structures. In the latter case it is obvious; in the former it is not so, but is yet traced. The existence and functions of life cannot be explained on exclusively mechanical principles. What is called mechanical energy is the effect and not the cause of vitality or vitivity or Shâkti as the Mother of all. The purpose of evolution is to take up the living potential from some lower grade, develop it and hand it over to a higher grade of forms.

Shakti as Chidânanda is, as Ichchhâ Shakti, the source of all forms of will-power and, in matter, of mechanical energy; and as Jnâna Shakti of all forms of mentality and feeling and as Kriyâ of all forms of activity (Kartrittva) being in itself all mighty.

The ultimate changeless Reality, in its aspect as Shâkti, veils and contracts in various degree its powers of will, knowledge and action. This veiling, negation, limitation, or contraction is seen at its fullest in so called "dead inert brute" matter. This allegation of lifeless inertia is however the result of superficial observation. It is true that in gross matter (Bhûta) the light of consciousness is turned down to its utmost. It is nowhere however even empirically extinguished. Chit is faintly manifested by scientific experiment in gross matter; more clearly in the micro-organisms between such matter and the vegetable world, in which, as in the animal world evolved from it, vitality is so obvious that we have been wont to call these alone "alive." Shâkta doctrine starts with the Full (Pûrna) and deals with the creation of things as a cutting down thereof. From a scientific point of view we may commence with the world as it is taking inorganic matter as the starting point. From such a standpoint we may speak (See "Vedas vital molecule" and "Notes on the radical vitality of all concrete matter" by G. Dubern) of a radical vital potential in all matter, universal, omnipresent, indestructible, all powerful; the source as will-power of mechanical energy, and as rudimentary sentiency of all mentality. From the Shâstric standpoint the process is one of veiling and unveiling. Shakti veils itself down to and in Prithivi Tattva of gross matter (Bhûta); and thereafter .

gradually unveils Herself up to and in man who in Samádhi realises his Svarûpa as pure, unveiled, Consciousness.

This veiling by Shákti takes place first in Shiva-Shakti Tattva by the complete negation of the "Idam" of experience ; and then through the action of the "Idam" on the subjective aspect of the consciousness of the pure creation, in which subject and object exist as part of the One self ; and then through that form of Shakti which is Máyâ which effects a severance of subject and object which are then experienced no longer as part of the one Self but as separate. The point of junction between Pure and Impure experience is the Tattva variously called Vidyâ, Sadvidyâ, or Shuddhavidyâ, the first truly realistic stage of the Yogî. Because it is in the intermediate state it is called Parâpara-dashâ (I'sh. Prat III 1-5) and as the Svachchhanda Tantra (IV, 95) says the "Experience in the form of Mantra of both difference and non-difference." After this Tattva, Máyâ intervenes.

In the Tattva Sandoha (v. 5) it is said " Máyâ is the sense of difference (Bhedabuddhi) in all Jîvas which are parts of Her. Just as the shore holds in the sea so she ever obstructs the manifestation (Vibhava) of Âtmâ which but for Her is otherwise unobstructed " (Máyâ vibheda-buddhir nijamsha-jûteshu nikhilajiveshu, Nityam tasya nirankusha-vibhavam veleva vâridhe rundhe).

So also in the I'shvara Pratyabhijnâ it is said "That which is nothing but the notion of difference (Bheda-dhi) in things entertained by the Doer (Karttâ) though in Himself of the nature of consciousness is Máyâ-Shakti, whom others, as in the case of Vidyeshvaras, call Vidyâ" (Bheda-dhîreva bhâveshu kartur bodhâtmano'piyâ, Máyâ shaktyeva sâ vidyetyanye vidyeshvarâ yathâ—III, ii, 6) "She is Vidyâ Shakti when She reveals in the Pashu state of the A'tmâ whose true nature is Lordship (Ishvaryya) but when She veils (Tirodhânakarî) then She is called Máyâ (Tasyaishvaryasvabhâvasya pashu-bhâve prakâshikâ, Vidyâ-Shaktîs-tirodhânakarî mâyâbhidhâ punah—ib. 7). Shiva has two functions namely Tirodhâna that by which He veils Himself to His worshipper and Anugraha where by He, through His grace, reveals Himself by the " descent of Shâkti " or grace (Shaktipâta). She is both .Madhumatî " Honey " and Máyâ (Lalitâ sahasranâma, v. 130). She is that saving (Târaka) knowledge by which the ocean of the Sangsâra is crossed. The Chitkalâ or Angsha of the great Consciousness enveloped by mind and matter is the Shakti which as the Padma Purâna says resides as the core of the " inner working " of all Jîvas and the Ânandakalikâ or germ of Bliss therein. She again as the Lalitâsahasranâma says (v142) is basis of the false (in the sense of impermanent) universe (Mithyâ Jagadishthânâ) created by, and which is, Her Mâyâ, the power of the Lord (Sândilya sûtra 86) which obscures and which, as the Shâkta Devî Purâna says, is called Mâyâ, because it is the marvellous instrument whereby unheard of results are produced like those of dreams or Magic. She is in all systems whether as Prakriti, Mâyâ or Mâyâ-shakti the finilising principle whereby forms are created in the formless Consciousness. This She effects by causing that duality of feeling of the self and not-self in the grand experience which is Mâhâsattâ. Under Her influence the Self experiences Itself as object in all the forms of the universe, which when completed is objectively seen as an evolution from Prakriti Tattva, that state of Shakti which is evolved by the action of Mâyâ and the five Kanchukas developed from Her. These are specific aspects of the great general limiting Power (Shakti) which Mâyâ is. With this Prakriti is associated Purusha Tattva, the two combined being Hangsa. Purusha Tattva is A'tmâ enveloped by the Kanchukas derived from Mâyâ and specific aspects of its operation. Shakti as Prakriti, subject to the influence of the Kanchukas, develops on the dis-equilibrium of Her Gunas from Herself as Vikritis the impure Tattvas (Ashuddha Tattva) extending to Prithivî. At this point conscious vital energy materialises forming what has been called by the author cited " the crust of the vital molecule " of all forms of solid matter. Subjectively therefore the Mâyâ process is the establishment of a dichotomy of subject and object in what would otherwise be an unitary experience ; and objectively it is the creation of the various psychical and physical forms into which the universal Substance projects ; becoming in the course of such emanation more and more gross. Bindu as the Mantra designation of Ishvara Tattva is Ghanibhûta ; that is the first Ghanâvasthâ aspect of Shakti becoming (through Mâyâ) Prakriti Tattva and its evolutes which are more and more gross (Sthûla) ; until passing the first four states of decreasing subltety of matter, Substance emerges as the solid atoms of matter which the physical universe is composed. These compounds being the subject of the senses are the material of physical science which seeks to work the process backwards. At a point, search on the path of objectivity is closed. If it would know more the mind must turn in on itself and release itself from all objectivity which Mâyâ is and fall back into that ground of Consciousness (Mâyâtitâ) whence it has emerged. From the Mantra aspect dealing with the origin of language the undifferentiated Shabda which arises on the differentiation of the Bindu into Purusha-Prakriti or Hangsa developes, with the creation of mind and matter, into the manifested Shabda and Artha which are the Varnas or letters (springing from the subtle Mâtrikâs) expressed in Vaikhari speech made up of letters (Varna) syllables (Pada) and sentences (Vâkya) of the uttered Mantra. Mantra again is the thought (*Man*) which saves (*Tra-Trayate*) : Saves from what ? From firstly the evil which man, subject to Mâvâ, commits ; and then, in the thorough purification of the mind (Chittashuddhi), from Mâyâ Herself who is transformed in the Sâdhaka into Vidyâ Shakti. Mantra is thus a pure thought-form; a pure Vritti or modification of the Antahkarana which is Devatâ. The senses and mind are also Devatâs being operations of the one Divine Shakti. Through Mantra the mind is divinely transformed. Contemplating, filled by, and identified with, Divinity in Mantra form, which is a Sthûla (gross) aspect of Devî. it passes into Her subtle (Sûkshma) Light form (Jyotirmayî Devî) which is the Consciousness beyond the world of Mâyik-forms ; the I'shvara and I'shvari who as Shabda-brahman are the source of, and appear as, that Mâyâ which is the Creatrix both of the objective world of Mind and Matter and of the manifested Shabda and Artha ; the Word and its Meaning derived from the Mother in Her aspect as Supreme Nâda (Paranâda) and Supreme Speech (Pâravâk).

THE KANCHUKAS.

The six Kanchukas including Mâyâ which may be regarded as the root of the other five are Kâla, Niyati, Râga, Vidyâ, Kalâ. The term Kanchuka means sheath or envelope. The same Tattvas are also called contractions (Sangkocha), for creation is the contracted (Sangkuchadrûpî) form of infinite Shakti. It is to be observed that Mâyâ, Niyati and Kâla, occupy in the philosophy of the Pancharâtra Âgama the very place which is held in the Shaiva-Shâkta system by the Kanchukas (See as to this Dr. Otto Schraders Ahirbudhnya Samhitâ 63, 64, 90). The author cited opines that the six Kanchukas are only an elaboration of the older doctrine of the three powers of limitation (Sangkocha) of the Pancharâtra which are Mâyâ, Kâla, Niyati. The same idea is expressed by these two terms, namely limitations by which the Âtmâ in its form as the finite experiencer is deprived of the specific attributes which It as the Perfect Experience possessed. Consciousness reaching forth to the World of enjoyment becomes subject to the Kanchukas and thus becomes the impure finite worldly experience where subject and object are completely different ; which experience is as it were, the *inversion* by the contraction and negation of Shakti of the perfect Experience from whose Shiva-Shakti Tattva aspect it proceeds. Infinite consciousness whilst still transcendentally retaining its Svarûpa is, as Shakti, narrowed to the degree which constitutes our experience on the material plane. The process may be represented in Diagram by an inverted triangle representing the Yoni or Shakti in the form of the Pure Tattvas resting on the point of an upright triangle. The point of intersection is Mâyâ from which proceeds the second triangle representing the impure Tattvas, which constitute worldly experience. Seen in the waters of Mâyâ all is reversed. Through the operation of Mâyâ and the Kanchukas, Shakti assumes the gross contracted form of Prakriti Tattva which in association with Purusha Tattva is Hangsa. Shiva and Shakti are the Bird Hangsa. Hangsa is both male (Pung or Purusha) and female (Prakriti). Hang is Shiva and Sah is Shakti. This Hangsa-dvanda are in their gross form the universe (Pung-prakrityâtmako hangsastadâtmakam idam jagat). Purusha is the Âtmâ enveloped by the Kanchukas which are the contractions of Consciousness and Its Powers. Mâyâ is the root and cause of all limitations of the powers (Vibhava) of consciousness (Âtmâ) ; for Mâyâ is the sense of difference (Bhedabuddhi) between all persons and things. Each Purusha, (and they are innumerable) being as the Svachchhanda Tantra says an universe of his own. Each Purusha creates under Mâyâ his or its own universe. The Kanchukas are thus the delimitations of the Supreme in Its form as Shakti. It was Eternity (Nityatâ) but is now orderly delimitation (Parichchheda) productive of appearance and disappearance (that is life and death). This is the operation of the Time-power or Kâla which is defined as follows in the Tattva-Sandoha (V. 7) "That Shakti of His which is Eternity (Nityatâ) descending and producing appearance and disappearance (birth and death) ; and which ever in regulated manner performs the function of division or delimitation (Parichchheda) should be regarded as in the form of Kâla Tattva."

(Sâ nityatâsya shaktir nikrishya nidhanodaya-pradânena, niyataparichchhedakari kliptâ syât Kâla-tattva-rûpena).

Kâla is the power which urges on and matures things. It is not in itself subjective or empirical time though it gives rise to it. It is transcendental Time without sections (Akhanda Kâla) giving birth to time as effect (Kâryyakâla). This gross time with parts (Sûkala Kâla) only comes in with the creation of the gross Tattvas. So it is said "Time leads me in time" (See Ahirbudhnya 64-67. See also the same Autho 's ueber den stand der Indischen Philosophic zur zeit Mahâvîras und Buddhas 17-30). Consciousness as Shakti is contracted into the mode of temporal thinking. It was freedom and independence (Svatantratâ). This is now contracted

3

and the Purusha is forcibly subjected to guidance and regulation
in what he must or must not do in any moment of time. This is
Niyati, which is defined in the Tattva Sandoha (v. 12) as follows :—
" That which constitutes that Shakti of His which is called Independence or Freedom (Svatantratà) ; this same Shakti, and none
other, becoming contracted and subjecting Him perforce to
guidance and regulation (Niyamayanti) in a definitely ordered and
restricted manner (Niyatam) as regards what is to be done or not
done (that is what he must not do at any given moment of time) is
Niyati."

(Yâsya svatantratûkhya-shaktih sangkochashâlinî saiva, krityâ-
krityeshvavashyam niyatam amûm niyamayantyabhûn niyatih).

Niyati is spoken of in the Pancharâtra Agama as the subtle
regulator of everything (Sûkshma-sarva-niyâmakah.) (Ahirbudhnya
VI. 46) and is said by Dr. Schrader (op-at 64, 65) to include in that
system the functions of the three Shaiva-Shâkta Kanchukas Vidyâ,
Râga and Kalâ (Ahirbudhnya S. 64-65). It was completely satisfied with Itself for there was then no other. It was the Full
(Pûrna), and there was nothing else for it to interest Itself in and
thus want. This Shakti, becoming limited, makes the Purusha
interested in objects and thus attaches them to enjoyment. This
is Râga which is defined in the Tattva Sandoha (v. 10) as
follows :—

" There is another Shakti of His which is eternal complete
satisfaction ; the same becoming limited and attaching him ever
to enjoyment, this Shakti is reduced to the condition of Râga-
tattva." (Nitya-paripûrna-tripti-shaktir asyaiva parimitâ nu satî,
bhogeshu ranjayati satatam amûm râga-tattvatâm yâ sâ). The
Brahman is, as the Isha Upanishad says, Pûrna the full, the all
which wants nothing ; for there is nothing to the All which It can
want. But when the one Experience becomes dual, and, subject
and object are separate, then the self as subject becomes interested
in objects that is in things other than itself. Ichchhà in the sense
of desire implies a want of the fullness which is that of the Supreme perfect experience. In the supreme creative sense Ichchhà is
the direction of Consciousness towards activity. The term Râga is
commonly translated desire. It is however properly that *interest* in
objects which precedes desire. Râga is thus that interest in objects
seen as other than the self which ripens into desire (Ichchhâ) for
them. Such Ichchhâ is thus a limitation of the all-satisfied fullness
of the Supreme.

The power of the Supreme was to know or experience all
things and so it is Sarvajnatâ. This is limited and the Purusha

thereby becomes a "little knower." This Kanchuka is called Vidyâ which is defined in the Tattva Sandoha (V. 9) as follows:— "His power of all-knowingness becoming limited and capable of knowing only a few things and producing knowledge (of a limited character) is called Vidyâ by the wise of old" (Sarvajnatâsya shaktih parimita tanur alpa-vedya-mâtra-parâ, jnânam utpâdayantîvidyeti nigadyate budhair âdyaih. *ibid* 9).

The supreme is all powerful, mighty to⁕ do all things (Sarvakartritâ). This power is contracted so that the Purusha can accomplish few things and becomes a "little Doer," This is Kalâ which is defined in the Tattva Sandoha (v. 8) as follows :—

" That which was His power of all-doing-ness, the same being contracted and capable of accomplishing but a few things and reducing him to the state of a little doer is called Kalâ." (Tat-sarvakârtritâ sâ samkuchitat katipayârtha-mâtra-parâ, Kinchit kartâram amum kalayantî kîrtyate kalâ nâma, *ibid*. 8). Kalâ is thus nothing but Kartrittva or infinite activity, agency, and mightiness cut down to the limits of the Jîvas' power ; that is lowered to the possibilities of finite action.

Thus the Shaktis of the Supreme which are many become contracted. Consciousness thus limited in sixfold manner by its own Shakti is the Purusha associated with Prakriti. Kalâ (in its more generic sense) is said in the Shaiva Tantrasâra (Âhnika 8) to be " the cause of the manifestation of Vidyâ and the root when she is operating on that Kartritva which is qualified by the qualifying conditions of littleness; this limited power of agency having been itself the work of Mâyâ. Now the moment that Kalâ separates from herself what constitutes this qualifying aspect spoken of above as Kinchit (little) at that very moment there is the creation of the Prakriti Tattva which is in the nature of a generality (Sâmânya-mâtra) unmarked by any specific form of object of enjoyment, such as happiness, sorrow and delusion ; and of which another name is the equalisation of the Gunas. Thus the creation under the influence of the Kalâ-tattva of the limited experiencer (Bhoktri) that is of the Purusha and of the experienced (Bhogya) or Prakriti is quite simultaneous that is without any succession whatever in the process. Thus being simultaneous they are ever associated."

The eighth Âhnika of the Taktrasâra (the Shaiva and not the Shâkta ritual work of Krishnânanda Âgamavâgîsha) says :—Thus it has been already shown that Kalâ is the cause of manifestation of Vidyâ and the rest (*i.e.*, the other four Kanchukas leaving out Mâyâ) when She (Kalâ) is operating on that agency or doer-ness (Kartritva) which is qualified (Visheshya) by the qualifying (Visheshana) condition of littleness; this limited power of agency (Kinchit-kartritva as opposed to Sarvva-kartritva) having been itself the work of Mâyâ. Now the moment that Kalâ separates from herself that which constitutes this qualifying aspect (Visheshana-bhâga) spoken of above as Kinchit and is an object of knowledge and action, that very moment there is the creation (Sarga) of the Prakriti-Tattva which is of the nature of a generality only (Sâmâ-nya-mâtra) unmarked by any specific forms of the enjoyable (Bhogya) such as happiness, sorrow, and delusion (which are there-fore as yet undifferentiated) and of which another name is the equalisation of their Gunas (i.e., of Sukha, Duhkha and Moha or of the Gunas of Her). Thus the creation under the influence of the Kalâ tattva of the Enjoyer (Bhoktri or limited experiencer) and Enjoyable (Bhogya or experienced) is quite simultaneous (that is without any succession whatever in the process and being simul-taneous they are conjoined. (Evam kinchit-kartritvam yan mâyâ-kâryam, tatra kinchitva-vishishtam yat kartrittvam visheshyam tatra vyâpriyamânâ kalâ vidyâdiprasavahetur iti nirûpitam. Idânîm visheshanabhâgo yah kinchid îiyukto jneyah kâryashcha tam yâvat sâ Kalâ svâtmanah prithak kurute tâvad esha eva sukha-duh-kha-mohâtmaka-bhogya-visheshânânusyûtasya sâmânya-mâtrasya tad-guna-sâmyaparanâmnah prakriti-tattvasya sargah ;—iti bhoktri-bhogya-yugalasya samam eva kalâ-tattvâyatâ srishtih).

Again in the Tantrâlokâ (Âhnika 9) it is said "So far it has been shown how Agency (Kartrittva) which is always accompanied by the power to enjoy (Bhoktritva) is (to be found) in that qualifi-ed aspect (that is Kartritva) of the Tattva called Kalâ which (aspect) is characterised by a limited agency (little doerness)."

Here may be interposed a note of explanation. Kartrittva is creative activity, ideation and formation as contrasted with a merely induced and passively accepted experience which is Jnâtritva Kartrittva is the power of modifying the Idam. The Sângkhyas say that the Purusha is Bhoktâ but not Kartâ. But the S'haiva-Shâktas hold that there is no Kartritva without Bhoktritva. In Parâsamvit there is the potential germ of (1) Jnâtritva, (2) Bhok-tritva (3) Kartrittva held in undistinguishable unity. In Shiva-Shakti Tattva the first exists and the second and third are through Shakti suppressed. In Sadâkhya there are the first and the incipiency of the second and third ; and in Ishvara Tattva all three are developed but as yet undifferentiate I. The Ishvara consciousness directed to the "Idam" produces equality of attention on "Aham" and "Idam" which is Sadvidyâ Tattva whence arise Mâyâ and the Kanchukas evolving Purusha-Prakriti. Parâsamvit is the pure

changeless aspect of Chit. Ishvara is the fully risen creative consciousness wherein is the undifferentiated Shakti which burgeons as
Ichchhâ, Jnâna, Kriyâ. Jnâtrittva or Jnâna Shakti in Ishvara does
not involve limited modification for the whole universe as the Self
is present to the Self. But in Purusha there is such modification ;
the Jnâtrittva functioning through Buddhi, the Vrittis of which are
expressions of the changing, limited, and partial characteristics of
the knowledge had through this instrument and its derivatives.

The citation continues. " But in what constitutes therein the
part " Kinchit " as a qualifying aspect, Kalâ gives birth to the
Pradhâna which arises from that (Kinchit aspect) as a clear but
general objectivity which is separate or distinct from (the Purusha).

Evam kalâkhya-tattvasya kinchit-kartrittva-lakshane,
Visheshyabhâge kartrittvam charchitam bhoktri-pûrvakam
Visheshanatayâ yo'tra kinchid bhâgas-tadûhitam,
Vedyamâtram sphutam bhinnam pradhânam sûyate kalâ.

That is Kartrittva is that aspect of Kalâ which is characterised
by Kinchit Kartrittva. From the qualifying (Visheshana that is
Kinchit) aspect Kalâ produces Prakriti which is distinct from Kalâ
as Purusha, which Prakriti exists as a mere general objectivity
which become particular when owing to disequilibrium in the
Gunas the Vikritis are produced.

Again it is said (ibid) " Kalâ produces the Bhogya (Prakriti)
and the Bhoktâ (Purusha) simultaneously by the notion of, or by
seeking for, a distinction (that is by seeking to establish a difference
between the two aspects in Herself namely Kartrittva and Kinchit ;
by working on Kartrittva alone), (yet), the Bhoktâ and Bhogya are
inseparate from one another. And because what is thus the barest
objectivity (Sangvedya-mâtra) is known (or experienced) later as [or
in the form of] happiness (Sukha) Sorrow (Duhkha) and delusion
(Vimoha) it is therefore called the equalisation of these (three) in
the beginning." (Samam hi bhogyang cha bhoktârang cha prasû-
yate Kalâ bhedâbhisandhânâd avyaktam parameshvaram, Evam
samvedyamâtram yat sukha-duhkha-vimohatah, bhotsyate yat tatah
proktam tat-sâmyâtmakam âditah).

When Mâyâ Shakti first severs the " Aham " and " Idam "
this latter is still experienced as an unlimited whole. The next step
is that in which the whole is limited and broken up into parts for
oar experience is not of an all pervading homogeneous whole but
of a heterogeneous universe. Kalâ, as a development of Mâyâ
Shakti, belittles the Purusha's hitherto unlimited Agency which
thus becomes Kinchit Kartrittva. Agency which exists both as to

the Knowable (Jneya) and object of action (Káryya) has two aspects, namely the qualified power of action (Visheshya Kartrittva) on the part of the Purusha and the object or "little" in respect of which Kartrittva operates, namely the "little" or universe (Kinchit or Visheshana) which is the "Idam" as viewed by Purusha after the opèration of Kalâ Shakti. Kalâ operates on agency (Kartrittva) and not on the "this" which is by such operation necessarily Kinchit. For if the power and experience of the Self is limited the object is experiehced as limited ; for the object is no'hing but the Self as obj-cf. In other words the production of Puru:ha is a positive operation of Kalâ whereas the production of Prakriti is a negative operation due to the limitation of the Purusha which as so limited experiences the universe as Kinchit. Prakriti is thus nothing but the object of Kartrittva as it exists when the la:ter has been whittled down by Kalâ. Purusha and Prakriti thus both emerge as the result of the action by Kalâ on the Purusha. For this reason Purusha and Prakriti are simultaneously produced and are also inseparable.

The following articles deal with Purusha and Prakriti or Hangsa ; the Kâmakalâ or three Bindus arising on the differentiation of the Parabindu which differentiation witnesses the birth of the Hangsa ; and lastly with the creation of the impure Tattvas (Ashuddha Tattva) from Prakriti and the Varnamâlâ the Garland or Rosary of letters, the evolution of which denotes the origin of speech and of Mantra.

HANGSA.

Hangsa is Purusha-Prakriti Tattva. Hang is "male" or Shiva ; Sah is "female" and Shakti. Shiva-Shakti are therefore Hangsa which combined mean the "Bird" Hangsa the material shape of which is variously said to be that of the goose, flamingo, brâhminî duck and by others to be legendary. The universe is made of and informed by this Hangsa Pair (Hangsadvanda) who are Purusha and Prakriti and in all the latter's varied forms (Pung-prakrityâtmako hangsa-stadâtmakam idam jagat). Of these the Anandalaharî says (39) "In Thy A âhata Lotus 1 salute the wondrous pair who are Hang aad Sah swimming in the mind of the great who ever delight in the honey of the blooming lotus of knowledge." That is they manifest in the mind of the great delight-ing in the honey of Consciousness. This Hangsa reversed is the Vedantic "So' ham" of which the Sammohana Tantra (Ch. VIII) says " Hakâra is one wing. Sakâra is the other. When stripped of both wings then Târa is Kâmakalâ." Jîva is Hangsa, The same Tantra says that the Sâlhaka of Târâ is the Lord of both Kâdi and Hâdi Mata. The Hangsatârâ Mahâvidyâ is the sovereign mistress of Yoga whom the Kâdis call Kâlî, the Hâdîs Shrîsundarî and the Kâdî-Hâdîs Hangsâ.

The Jnânârnava Tantra (xxi-vv i-9) speaking of the Chitkunda as the Mandala in the Mûlâdhâra where Homa is done, defines as follows the four Âtmâs, *viz.*, Paramâtmâ ; Antarâtmâ, Jnânatmâ and Âtmâ which form the Chitkunda and by the knowledge whereof there is no rebirth. Âtmâ is Prânarûpî that is the Âtmâ which is in all beings as their Prâna, It is Hangsa Svarûpî or Jîvâtmâ manifested by outer and inner ! reathing (Shvâsa, uchchhvâsa). It is compared to the ether in a pot which the potter's wheel separates from the surrounding Akâsha but from which there is no distinction when the pot is broken. The individual breath is the cosmic breath from which it seems to be different by the forms which the latter vitalises. Jnânâtmâ is Sûkshât-sâkshi-rûpaka. It is that which witnesses all and by which the unity of all is known. It is reflected in Buddhi and the rest and is yet in its own form distinguishable therefrom, just as the rays of the moon are reflected on water and seem to be, and are yet not, one with it. It is thus the substratum of Buddhi and of all the subjective or mental Tattvas derivable therefrom. By " Antar " in the term Antarâtmâ is meant the subtle (Rahasya-sûkshmarûpaka) Âtmâ which pervades all things ; the spark of Paramâtmâ which indwells all bodies (Antargata). It is the Hangsa known only by Yogîs. Its beak is Târâ (Prânava or "Om" Mantra). Nigama and Âgama are its two wings. Shiva and Shakti its two feet. The three Bindus are its three eyes. This is the Paramahangsa; that is Hangsa in its supreme aspect as the Consciousness-ground of the manifested Hangsa or Jîva. When this Paramahangsa is spread (Vyâpta) that is displayed, then all forms of matter (Bhûta), *viz.*, Âkâsha, Pavana and the rest spring up in their order. Of these five the root is Chitta. This Hangsa disports itself in the world-lotus sprung from the Mud of Delusion (Mohapangka) in the Lake of Ignorance (Avidyâ). When this Hangsa becomes unworldly (Nishprapancha) and in dissolving-form (Sanghârarûpa) then it makes visible the Âtmâ or Self (Âtmânam pradirshayet). Then its " Birdness" (Pakshâitva) disappears and the Soham Âtmâ is established. " Know this " says the Jnânârnava "to be the Paramâtmâ."

Purusha is Âtmâ subject to Mâyâ Shakti and the other limiting Shaktis called the Kanchukas. Prakriti is that state of Shakti which arises as the result of the collective operation of Máyá and the Kanchukas ; a transformation of Shakti which is their result existing as a homogeneity and general objectivity which develops of its own power which is the summation of the Shaktis producing it, into the heterogeneous universe. The Purusha-Prakriti Tattvas arise as a bifurcation in consciousness on the differentiation of the Parabindu into the three Bindus which form the Kámakalá which again may be pictured as the triangular base of the pyramidal (Shringátaka) figuré in the Shrî Yantra at whose apex is the Baindava Chakra and Parabindu. The three Bindus represent the Shiva aspect and the Shakti aspect of the one Consciousness, and the third the mutual relation or Shiva-Shakti aspect of the two. From this differentiation arises in the Mantra-line of creation Parashabda and manifested Shabda and Artha ; in the Tattva line Buddhi and the rest ; and in the line of the Lords of the Tattvas (Tattvesha) Shambhu and the rest. In its most general and philosophical sense Purusha-Prakriti represent that stage in the evolving consciousness (Shakti) in which after passing from the mere I-experience (Ahampratyayavimarsha) and the "I-this" or "Aham-idam" experience in which the object or Idam is still experienced as part of the self (the completed type of such ex- periencer being Ishvara), Consciousness emerges as the experience of duality in which the object is seen as outside of, and separate from, the self. This however is a state of mere general objectivity. The final state has yet to be described when undifferentiated objectivity and supreme Sound (Parashabda) evolves, the first into the differentiated objects of the universe (Ashuddha Tattva) and the second into the differentiated word (Shabda) and its meaning (Artha) which is the birth of Mantra consisting of letters (Varna), syllabies (Pada) and sentences (Vákya). With the differentiation of Prakriti appear multitudinous Purushas of varying experience each living in an universe of its own.

Purusha is not merely confined to man but is applicable to every Jîva who is the Enjoyer (Bhoktá) or Purusha of the enjoy- able (Bhogya) or Prakriti. Purusha again is not limited to the organic life of animals and plants or the micro-organisms which hover between organic and inorganic matter. The term includes the latter also. For whatever may be the popular signification of the term Jîva as living organic bodies, in its philosophical sense all is Jivátmá which is not Paramátmá. And in this, modern science bears out the notions here described. The former arbitrary parti- tions made between the living and non-living are being broken down. We may for practical purposes call that " living " which

obviously displays certain characteristics which we call " life"
such as the so-called vital phenomena manifested by plants,
animals and men. But the life and consciousness displayed in
organic bodies is not something wholly new which had no existence
in the inorganic material of which they are composed. All such
vital phenomena exist in subdued or potential form in every kind of
matter which contains the potentiality of all life. Life as we know
it is the phenomenal aspect of Being-Itself (Sat). Feeling-
Consciousness as we know it is the limited manifestation (manifestation being limitation) of the undifferentiated Feeling-Consciousness
which is Chit, Sat and Ananda. All which is manifested exists
potentially in its ground. Each of such manifestations is such
ground (Bhûmi) veiled in varying degrees ; now more, now less
fully displaying the nature of Spirit, the source of all life, feeling,
will, and consciousness. Superficial notions based on appearances
have given rise to the notion of "dead" matter. But science
has given new instruments for, and extended the range of, our
observation and has shown that life and consciousness, though in
a subdued or veiled form, exists throughout the universe. Vedânta
in its Shâkta version says that all forms are the operation of
Consciousness as Mâyâ-Shakti. As the ancient Upanishad says
and modern so-called " New thought" repeats "What one thinks
that one becomes." All recognise this principle to a certain point.
If man thinks inhuman thoughts he dehumanises himself. Vedânta
carries the application of this principle to its logical conclusion
and affirms that not only does thought operate modifications in
and within the limits of particular types or species, but actually
evolves such and all other types through the cosmic or collective
Thought of which the universe is a material expression. Thus
every unit or atom of matter is a Purusha identifying itself with the
solid (Pârthiva) " crust" of matter which is the gross expression on
the sensual plane of more subtle forces emanating from that
Ground Substance which is the source both of the experiencing
subject and the object experienced. If the operation of gross
matter gives the appearance of rigid mechanism, this does not
imply that such operation is wholly unconscious and lifeless but
that life and consciousness are veiled by the Tamas Guna of
Prakriti in which Kalâ, Niyati and other Kanchukas are operating
to their fullest extent. But however intense may be their operation,
life and consciousness can,never be destroyed, for being Shakti
Herself they are indestructible. Thus every molecule of mineral
substance is a Purusha or Consciousness identifying itself with
matter in its solid and apparently unconscious and inert state.
For Consciousness becomes that with which it identifies itself, .

When it completely identifies itself with mineral matter it becomes that matter. What we think that we become. Nothing however is absolutely unconscious or inert. Every single atom in the universe is in constant movement and hence the world is called Jagat or that which moves. This scientific doctrine is in India an ancient inheritance. And so the Mantra runs " Hring the Supreme Hangsa dwells in the brilliant Heaven." The word Hangsa is here said to be derived from the word Hanti which means Gati or motion. Sâyana says that it is called Âditya because it is in perpetual motion.

The Tattva Sandoha (vv. 13, 14) says :—

" She is considered to be Prakriti who is the collectivity of all the Shaktis, (Will, Knowledge and Action) who is the peaceful that is quiescent (Shântâ) Shakti of Him in contracted form (Samkuchadrûpâ) ; who is in the form of the equilibrium of Sattva, Rajas and Tamas Gunas which again are Will, Knowledge and Action gathered together (Samkalita) ; who is in the nature of general unparticularised feeling (Chitta) which is in the form of the undifferentiated Buddhi (and other Tattvas)."

(Ichchhâdi-shakti-samashtih shaktih shântâsya samkuchadrûpâ, Samkalitechchhâdyâtmaka - sattvâdika - sâmya-rûpinî hi sati, Buddhyâdi-sâmarasya-svarûpâ chittâtmikâ matâ prakritih).

" Hang " or the male (Pumân) or Purusha is again in the same work (V. 6) described as :—

" He who having by Her become of limited form with all His powers contracted is this Male (Pumân or Purusha) ; like the sun which becoming red at eventide and His power (of shining) contracted can scarce reveal himself (by shining abroad)" (Sa tayâ parimitamûrtih samkuchita-samasta-shaktir eshah pumân, Kaviriva sandhyâ-rakta-samhrita-shaktih svabhâsane' pyapatuh. Ibid. 6).

Again in the same work (v. 7) it is said :—

" His Shaktis are many consisting of complete Kartritivä (power of action) and others, but on His becoming contracted (that is limited) they also become contracted in the forms of Kalâ and the rest and make him thus manifest (as Purusha) (Sampûrma-kartritvâdyâ bahvyah santyasya shaktaya stasya, Samkochât samkuchitâh kalâdi rûpena rûdhayantyevam. Ibid, 7.)

Again in the Ishvara Pratyabhijnâ it is said :—

" He who is Experiencer commencing with Shûnya (Shiva-tattva) and the rest, He being clothed by the five Kanchukas, Kâla and the rest, and becoming object (to himself) is then the Experiencer of objects as separate from him;" (Yashcha pramâtâ shuniyâdih prameye vyatirekhini, Mâtâ sa meyah san kâlâdika-panchakaveshtitah-III-il 9), that is object-is the Self appearing as such. He retains His own Self-hood and becomes at the same time the object of His own experience. Mâyâ is not something apart from Brahman for it is Brahman who through Mâyâ, an aspect of Brahman, becomes Himself His own object. In the first act of creation He commences to become His own object, but it is only when the subject as Purusha is clothed, that is limited, • by the Kanchukas, that the latter sees objects as other than and outside Himself. At this stage duality is established and exfoliates in the Vikritis of Prakritis as the multiple experience of the World of Mind and Matter.

The Gunas of Prakriti are inadequately translated as qualities because the latter word involves some Substance of which they are the qualities. But Prakriti Shakti is as Prakriti the Gunas and nothing else, though Her Svarûpa, as that of all Shaktis, is Sat-Chit-Ânanda. The Gunas Sattva, Rajas, Tamas are properly factors or constituents of Prakriti. Of these it is commonly said that Tamas Guna is the veiling principle of Prakriti. This is so. But nevertheless it is to be remembered that all the factors of Prakriti in one way or another veil ; the difference being that whereas Sattva to some degree veils (for Sattva guna is not as such the same as absolute Sat) it is in its highest degree of potency that is predominance, the least degree of veiling and therefore it represents the tendency to unveil that is to reveal and manifest Being (Sat) and Consciousness (Chit) ; whereas Tamas is in its highest potency the greatest degree of veiling and therefore specifically represents the tendency to veil. Rajas is the operative power in both cases. In all bodies there are the three Gunas (for these cannot separately exist though one or other may predominate) and it is because of this and therefore of the presence of Sattva Guna in inorganic matter that it exhibits the rudiments of sentiency and consciousness. But in inorganic matter Tamas Guna prevails. As bodies evolve, the strength of the operation of Tamas gradually diminishes and that of Sattva increases until in man it becomes predominant. The whole object of Sâdhanâ is to increase Sattva Guna until man becoming wholly Sâttvik his body*passes from the state of predominant Sattva Guna into Sat Itself. These Gunas represent in the Jîva or Pashu the Ichchhâ, Kriyâ, Jnâna and Mâyâ Shaktis of the Lord. As regards Mâyâ, the Lord (Mâyin), as the Kulârnava Tantra says, wields and controls and is free of it ; Jîva is .

controlled by it. So the Ishvara-Pratyabhijnâ `(IV. 1, 4) says
" What are Jnâna and Kriyâ (on the part) of the Lord (Pati) in
all beings and things (Bhâveshu) (which to Him are really) of the
nature of (His) own body (or limbs)—it is these two (that is Jnâna
and Kriyâ) and nothing else (eva) which together with Mâyâ as
the third are the Sattva, Rajas, and Tamas (Gunas in respect) of
the Pashu" (Svânga-rupeshu bhâveshu patyurjnânam kriyâ cha yâ,
Mâyâ-tritaye te eva pashoh sattvam rajas tamah)

Shiva-Shakti have threefold aspect as Ichchhâ, Jnâna, Kriyâ
which are inseparably associated just as the Gunas are, though as
in the latter case one or other may be predominant. Of these again
Ichchhâ and Kriyâ may be considered together ; for as resolve is
directed to action it is the preliminary of it. Ichchhâ in the
Shaiva Shâstra is described as a state of wonder (Sâ chamatkâra-
ichchhâ shaktih) in the Purusha. But Kriyâ considered (for the
purpose of analysis only) as apart from Jnâna is blind. For this
reason Kriyâ has been associated with Tamas. It is very
clearly explained by Kshemarâja in his Tattva Sandoha (vv. 13-15)
that Ichchhâ or resolve to action becomes at a lower stage Rajas
Guna the principle of activity in Prakriti ; Jnâna becomes Sattva
or the principle of manifestation in the same ; and Kriyâ becomes
Tamas guna or the specific veiling principle of the same form of
Shakti. He says " His Will (Ichchhâ) assumed the form of Rajas
and became Ahangkâra which produces the notion of "I" (Aham).
His knowledge (Jnâna) likewise became Sattvarûpa and Buddhi
which is the determining form of experience. His Kriyâ being in
the nature of Tamas and productive of Vikalpa (and Sangkalpa) i.e.,
rejection and selection is called Manas " (Ichchhâsya rajo-rûpâham-
kritir âsid aham-pratîtikarî jnanâpi (should be Jnânamapi)
sattvarûpâ nirnayabodhasya kâranam buddhih, Tasya kriyâ
tamomaya-mûrtir mana uchyate vikalpakarî),

The evolution of these Tattvas (Ashuddha) is the subject of a
future article. But before dealing with these it is necessary, in the
creative order, to further describe the Kâmakalâ in which the
Hangsa arises and the Rosary or Garland of letters (Varnamâlâ)
which is the Mantra aspect of the Tattvik evolution.

THOMPSON AND CO., PRINTERS, MADRAS.

STUDIES

IN

MANTRA SHÂṢṬRA

PART IV

, (Kâmakalâ, The gross Tattvas and their Lords, The Garland

of Letters or Varnamâlâ.)

BY

ARTHUR AVALON

December 1918

(Reprinted from the " Vedanta Kesari")

PRINTED BY
THOMPSON AND CO., AT THE " MINERVA " PRESS,
33, POPHAM'S BROADWAY, MADRAS.

STUDIES IN THE MANTRA SHÂSTRA.

(KÂMAKALÂ).

BY

ARTHUR AVALON.

In the previous articles it has been shown that the Parabindu
or Ishvara Tattva assumes in creation a threefold aspect as the
three Bindus,—Bindu (Kâryya) Nâda, Bîja. These three points
constitute symbolically a Triangle which is known as the Kâmakalâ. Kâma is of course not here used in the gross sense of desire,
sexual or otherwise, but of Ichchhâ the Divine creative Will towards
the life of form which is here explicated from Bindu the aspect
previously assumed by Shakti through Nâda (Bindutâm abhyeti).
The undivided supreme Chit shakti (Akhandaparachichchhakti)
becoming desirous of appearing as all the Tattvas (Samastatattva-
bhâvena vivarttechchhâsamanvitâ) assumes the Bindu aspect (Bindu-
bhâvang paryeti) characterised by a predominance of activity
(Kriyâprâdhânyalakshanâ). Here it may be observed that Ichchhâ
or Will is a form of Kriyâ (action): in the sense that it is the preliminary to action and sets the Self in motion. Shakti passes from
potency through Will to action which through Para Bindu manifests.
Bindubhâva is that state (Ishvaratattva) in which it is fully equipped to work and does so. Its threefold aspect as it works are
Bindu Shivâtmaka, Bîja shaktyâtmaka and Nâda is Samavâya
that is relationship or connection (Sambandha) as exciter (Kshobhaka) and that which is excited, (Kshobhya) which relation is the
cause of creation (Srishtihetu). The Shâradâ (1. 10) then proceeds to deal with the appearance of the three Devîs and three
Devas which are in the nature of the three Shaktis (Ichchhâ, etc.)
and Fire, Moon and Sun. Having then dealt with Shabdasrishti
it proceeds to describe Arthasrishti (1. 15) giving first the line of
Devas from Shambhu who are the Lords of the Tattvas (Tattvesha) and then that part of Arthasrishti which is Tattvasrishti or
the evolution of the Tattvas of mind and matter from Buddhi to
Prithivî.

It is not easy in all cases to discover and set forth an accurate
summary of the Devîs, Devas, Shaktis and so forth in Shabdasrishti;
because the texts being in verse are not always to be read as they

stand, the order of words being in some cases regulated by the
metre. As the author of the Prânatoshinî says in dealing with a
citation from the Goraksha Samhitâ, that the texts must not be read
" Pratishabdam" that is according to the order of the words but
" Yathâsambhavam" according to the facts. But this does not
relieve us from the difficulty of ascertaining what is the fact ; that
is, the real order. Other elements may also enter into the calcula-
tion : for instance, as Râghava Bhatta points out, the order of
Shaktis varies in Ishwara and Jîva. In the former it is Ichchhâ,
Jnâna, Kriyâ and in Jîva Jnâna, Ichchhâ, Kriyâ. In Ishvara's
ideation (Pratyabhijnâ) when He desires to do anything,
an act of volition proceeds from Him (Svechchhayâ kriyâ) to
know or to do it (Tat jnâtung kartung vâ) ; next there is the
capacity for cognising such acts (Tat kâryyajnânadarshana-
shaktitâ) which is Jnâna-shakti ; thirdly the gross effort (Sthûlah
samudyamah) is the Kriyâ shakti (Kriyâshaktirudîtâ) from which
the whole world proceeds (Tatah sarvang jagat param). Râghava
also points out that there is a difference of order in Shabdasrishti
and Arthasrishti. Thus in dealing with the Pranava it is said " A
which is Sun is Brahmâ :" but here in the Shâradâ verse, Vishnu
is Sun. I will first give the order as it is given in the Shâradâ
Text. (v. 10) " From Bindu came Raudrî ; from Nâda Jyeshthâ,
from Bîja, Vâmâ. From these came Rudra, Brahmâ, Ramâdhipa
(Vishnu).

Raudrî bindostato nâdât jyeshthâ bîjâd ajâyata

Vâmâ, tâbhyah samutpannâ rudrabrahmaramâdhipâh.

It then continues " Who are in the nature of Jnâna, Ichchhâ,
Kriyâ and Fire, Moon and Sun (v. 11).

(Sangjnânechchhâ kriyâtmâno vahnîndvarkasvarûpinah) who
are in the form (Rûpa) of Nirodhikâ, Arddhendu and Bindu.
These are all different states of Shakti (Shakterevâvasthâ-visheshâh),
for it is owing to their arising from Shakti (Shaktitah utpannatvât,
that they are identified with the Shaktis Ichchhâ and so forth.

According to the Yoginîhridaya Tantra (1) the order is (a)
Ichchhâ-Vâmâ-Pashyantî; (b) Jnâna-Jyeshthâ-Madhyamâ; (c) Kriyâ,
Raudrî-Vaikharî. It says that when Ichchhâ Shakti in the form
of a goad (Angkushâkâra ; that is the bent line Vakrarekhâ) is
about to display the universe which is in seed (Bîja) form She is
Vâmâ and in the form of Pashyantî shabda. Pashyantî = " She who
sees" Îkshana. Vâmâ is so called because this Shakti vomits forth
the universe (Vamanât Vâmâ). Jyeshthâ which is in the form of

a straight line (Ŗijurekhâ) attaining the state of Mâtrikâ (Matrikâ-
tvam upapannâ) is Madhyamâ vâk. Kaudrî is Kriyâ in triangular or
pyramidal (Shringâtaka) that is three-dimensional form and is the
manifested Vaikharî Shabda. According to the Kâmakalâ vilâsa
(Comm. v. 22) Yoginîhridaya Tantra (Sangketa 1) and the Saubhâ-
gyasudhodaya (cited in Sangketa 2 of the last Shâstra) the order
would appear to be (a) Ichchhâ-Rajas-Vâmâ-Brahmâ-Pashyanti
Shabda ; (b) Jnâna-Sattva-Jyeshthâ-Vishnu-Madhyamâ Shabda ; (c)
Kriyâ-Tamas-Raudrî-Rudra-Vaikharî Shabda.

I will not however here attempt a discussion which would be
both lengthy and technical of the texts on this point. For practical
present purposes it is sufficient to know that the three Bindus are
Shiva, Shakti, Shiva-shakti ; Prakâsha, Vimarsha, Prakâsha-
vimarsha ; White, Red and Mixed ; Bindu, Nâda, Bîja ; Supreme,
Subtle, Gross ; the three Devîs, the three Devas, and the three
Shaktis of Will, Knowledge and Action. The Supreme at this
point thus becomes a Trinity of Energy.

The division of the Mahâbindu may be memorised by writing
in Sanskrit the " Fire" Bîja or Ram : that is Ra with Chandrabindu (र). Then invert the Nâda sign which will thus represent
the Moon (Indu), the Bindu, the Sun (Ravi), and the Ra, Fire
(Agni). The Triangle may be formed by drawing two sides or a
bent line and then completing it with a straight line. At the apex
place the ⸲ Ravibindu (Sun) and at the left and right hand corners
Vahnibindu (Fire) and Moon (Chandrabindu). Between Sun and
Moon place Vâmâ Vakrarekhâ and Brahmâ ; between Fire and
Moon, Jyeshthâ and Vishnu ; and between Moon and Sun Raudrî
Rijurekhâ and Rudra. Between each of the points are lines formed
by all the letters (Mâtrikâ varna) of the alphabet called the A-Ka-
Tha triangle. The Pâdukâpanchaka, a Hymn attributed to Shiva,
(Tantrik Texts, Vol. 2) speaks of A-Ka-Tha in the second verse on
which Kâlîcharana comments as follows :—Here He is Kâmakalâ in form and the three Shaktis (Vâmâ, Jyeshthâ, Raudrî) emanating from the three Bindus are the three lines. The sixteen
vowels beginning with A form the line Vâmâ, the sixteen letters
beginning with Ka from the line Jyeshthâ and the sixteen
letters beginning with Tha form the line Kaudrî. . The abode of
Shakti (Abalâlayam) is formed by these three lines. The other
three letters Ha, La, Ksha are in the corners of the Triangle.
Kâlîurdhvâmnâya says " The Tribindu is the Supreme Tattva
and embodies in itself Brahmâ, Vishnu, Shiva (Brahmavishnushi-
vâtmakam). The Triangle composed of the Letters has emanated
from the Bindu;" also " The letters A to Visargah make the line

Brahmâ, the letters Ka to Ta the line Vishnu, and the letters Tha to Sa the line Rudra. The three lines emanate from the three Bindus. The Gunas, as aspect of Shakti, are also represented by this threefold division. The Tantrajîvana says " The lines Rajas, Sattva, Tamas surround the Yonimandala " Also " above is the line of Sattva, the line of Rajas is on its left and the line of Tamas on its right." .

The Shabdabrahman in its threefold aspect and Energies is represented in the Tantras by this triangular Kâmakalâ which is the abode of Shakti (Abalâlaya). The Triangle is in every way an apposite symbol, for on the material plane if there are three forms there is no other way in which they can be brought to interact except in the form of a triangle in which whilst they are each, as aspects, separate and distinct from one another, they are yet related to each other and form part of one whole. In the Âgamakalpadruma it is said that the Bindu is Hang (one point) and Visargah (two points) is Sah or Shakti. The Yâmala thus speaks of this abode " I now speak of Kâmakalâ" and proceeding says " She is the Eternal One who is the three Bindus the three Shaktis and the three Forms (Trimûrtti). The Mâheshvarî Sambitâ says Sun, Moon and Fire are the three Bindus and Brahmâ, Vishnu, Rudra the three lines. The Lalitâsahasranâma calls the Devî, Kâmakalârûpâ. Bhâskararâya in his commentary thereon (v. 78) says that Kâma or creative will (Ichchhâ) is both Shiva and Devî and Kalâ is their manifestation. Hence it is called Kâmakalâ. This is explained in the Tripura-siddhânta " Oh Parvatî, Kalâ is the manifestation of Kâmeshvara and Kâmeshvarî. Hence She is known as Kâmakalâ. Or She is the manifestation (Kalâ) of Desire (Kâma) that is of Ichchhâ Shakti. The Devî is the great Tripurasundarî. Bhâskararâya's Guru Nrisinghânandanâtha wrote the following verse on which the disciple comments :

" I Hymn Tripurâ, the treasure of Kula, who is red of beauty ; Her limbs like unto those of Kâmarâja who is adored by the three Devatâs of the three Gunas ; who is the desire or Will of Shiva (according to the Anekârthadhvanimanjarî lexicon I = Manmatha = Kâma Ichchhâ) who dwells in the Bindu and who manifests the Universe." She is red because she is the Vimarshashakti. She is called (says the Commentator cited) Tripurâ as She has three (Tri) Puras (literally cities or abodes) here meaning three Bindus, lines, angles, syllables and so forth. She has three angles (in the triangular Yoni the source of the universe) as well as three circles (the three Bindus) and the Bhûpura of Her Yantra has three lines.

Yoni does not here mean generative organ but Kâranam the Cause of the universe. She has three aspects and creates the three Devatâs through the three Shaktis Vâmâ and others and manifests as Will, Knowledge and Action. Thus since She the Supreme Energy is everywhere triple she is called Tripurasundarî. The three syllables of Her Mantra are the three divisions of the Panchadashî namely Vâgbhava, Kâmarâja and Shakti Kûtas which according to the Vâmakeshvara Tantra are the Jnâna and other Shaktis. The Kâmabîja is Klîng and Klîngkâra is Shivakâma. Here "I" is said to denote the Kâmakalâ in the Turîya state through which Moksha is gained and hence the meaning of the saying that "he who hears the Bija without Ka and La does not reach the place of good actions"—that is he does not go to the region attainable by good actions but to that (Moksha) attainable by Jnâna alone. The Bhâvachûdâmani says " Meditate on the face in the form of Bindu, and below on the twin breasts (the two other Bindus) and below them the beauteous form of the Hakârârddha. The commentator on the Ânandalaharî says " In the fifth sacrifice (Yajna) let the Sâdhaka think of his Âtmâ as in no wise different from, but as the one and only, Shiva ; and of the subtle thread-like Kundalinî who is all Shaktis extending from the Âdhâra Lotus to Paramashiva. Let him think of the three Bindus as being in Her body indicating Ichchhâ, Jnâna, Kriyâ ; Moon, Sun, Fire ; Rajas, Sattva, Tamas ; Brahmâ, Vishnu, Rudra : and then let him meditate upon the Chitkalâ who is Shakti below it ". The Bindu which is the " Face " indicates Virinchi (Brahmâ) associated with the Rajas Guna. The two Bindus which are the " Breasts " and upon which meditation should be done in the heart indicate Hari (Vishnu) and Hara (Rudra) associated with the Sattva and Tamas Gunas. Below then meditate upon the subtle Chitkalâ which indicates all three Gunas and which is all these three Devatâs. Similar meditation is given in Yoginî (and other) Tantras winding up with the direction ·· and then let the Sâdhaka think of his own body as such Kâmakalâ."

As regards this it is to be observed that in the Mûlâdhâra there is a Traipura Trikona so-called because of the presence of the Devî Tripurâ within the Ka inside the triangle. This Ka is the chief letter of the Kâma Bîja and Kang is the Bîjâ of Kâminî, the aspect of Tripurasundarî in the Mûlâdhâra. Here also are the three lines, Vâmâ, Ichchhâ and so forth. Thus the Traipura Trikona is the Sthûla aspect of the Sûkshma shakti in the region of the upper Sahasrâra called Kâmakalâ. It is to this Kâminî that in worship the essence of japa (Tejorûpajapa) is offered, the external japa being given to the Devatâ worshipped in order that the Sâdhaka may retain the fruits of his Japa (Nityapûjâpaddhati 8). Man physically and psychically is a limited manifestation of this threefold Shakti which resides within himself and is the object of worship. Such, worship leads to identification and so the Shrîtattvârnava says " Those glorious men who worship in that Body in Sâmarasya are freed from the waves of poison in the untraversable sea of the universe (Sangsâra)". Sâmarasya I may here observe is a term which is ordinarily applied to the bliss of sexual union (Strîpungyogât yat saukhyang tat sâmarasyam). For the benefit however of those who are always reading gross meanings into parts of the Shâstra alien to them it is necessary to explain that Sâmarasya is both gross (Sthûla) and subtle (Sûkshma). Here the latter is meant. An erotic symbol is employed to denote the merger of the Jîva and Supreme Consciousness in ecstasy (Samâdhi). The Tantras largely employ such imagery which is to be found in the Upanishads and in non-Indian scriptures. Thus the highly sensual imagery of the Biblical " Song of Songs" is said (whether rightly or not, I will not here inquire) to symbolise Christ's love for His Bride the Church. Spiritual union is symbolised by terms borrowed from the world of man. By Mantrayoga is sought that perfection and unity of Bhâva which leads to Jnânayoga Samâdhi.

" On the division of the Supreme Bindu (into the threefold Kâma-kalâ) there was Unmanifested Sound" (Bhidyamânât parâdbindoravyaktâtmaravo bhavat (Shâradâ-l-11). This is the Shabdabrahman or the Brahman as the cause of manifested Shabda and Artha and therefore of Mantra. This causal "Sound" is the unmanifested (Avyaktâtmâ) undifferentiated (Akhanda) principle of Shabda (Nâdamâtra) composed of Nâda and Bindu (Nâdabindumaya) devoid of all particularity such as letters and the like (Varnâdivishesha-rahita). Some as the Shâradâ says (V. 12) have thought that the Shabdabrahman was Shabda and others Shabdârtha but this cannot be Jor both are unconscious (Jadatvât) " In my opinion" its author says (v. 13) " Shabdabrahman is the Consciousness in all beings" (Chaitanyang sarvvsbhûtânâng shabdabrahmeti me matih). For if Shabdârtha or Shabda be called Shabdabrahman then the meaning of the term Brahman is lost (Brahmapadavâchyatvang nopapadyate) ; for the meaning of the term Brahman (Brahmapadârtha)' is Sat-Chit-Ânanda (Sachchidânandarûpa) whilst these are unconscious (Jada). Râghava Bhatta says that Shabdabrahman is 'Nâdabindumaya Brahman (Brahmâtmaka) sound (Shabda) unmanifested (Avyakta) undifferentiated (Akhanda) all pervading (Vyâpaka) which is the first manifestation of Paramashiva in creative mood (Srishtyunmukhaparamashivaprathamollasamatram). He also cites a passage from some work unnamed which says that out of Prakriti in Bindu form in whom Kriyá Shakti prevails (Kriyàshaktipradhânâyâh prakriter bindu-rûpinyàh) arose the Supreme Shabdabrahman the cause of Shabda and Shabdártha (Shabdashabdârthakâranam). The Sound (Rava) here spoken of is in the form of Bindu (Bindurûpa) which later appears in all bodies as the Mâtrikâs and, Varnas in their respective places. The Shâradâ (I. 14) having thus dealt with Parâshabdasrishti concludes in a general way "Consciousness which is the Svarûpa of, and appears as, Kundali Shakti in the bodies of all living beings manifests as Letters in prose and verse having obtained the instruments for utterance which are the throat and so forth."

Tat prâpya kunoalirûpang prâninâng dehamadhyagam
Varnâtmanàvirbhavati gadyapadyàdibhedatah.

The subsequent Shabdasrishti is derived from Kundalinî. The Kâmakalâ is thus called the root (Mûla) of all Mantra for it is the threefold aspect of the Shabdabrahman the cause of all manifested Shabda and Artha and therefore of Mantra. In a future article I will continue the account of the creative process, namely, the Arthasrishti in which are included the Tattvas from Buddhi to Prithivî and the Lords (Tattvesha) or forms of Consciousness which preside over them. These are necessarily dealt with in connection with the Tattvas over which they preside. In the same way Pashyantî, Madhyamâ, and Vaikharî states of sound are here also dealt with because Pashyantî and the others only exist in the created body. Parashabda is unmanifested Chaitanya but the other Three Feet of the One Brahman are set in the manifested world of Mind and Matter.

THE GROSS TATTVAS AND THEIR LORDS.

The Shâradâ Tilaka (Chapter I) having first dealt with Shabdasrishti on account of its priority (Prâdhânyadyotanâya prathamoddishtam) commences with the fifteenth verse to speak of the creation of objects (Arthasrishti), for Pashyantî and the other Bhâvas assume the existence of the manifested body. It says from Shambhu who is in the nature of Kalâ (Kalâtmanah) and Bindu (Bindvâtmanah) and friend of Kâla (Kâlabandhu) issued (Ajâyata) the "Witness of the World" (Jagatsâkshî), the all pervading (Sarvavyâpî) Sadâshiva. Râghava says Kalâ is here either used generally, or as referring to the Nivritti and other Kalâs which Shambhu produces. By "friend of Kâla" is meant that Shambhu is in the nature of Nâda (Nâdâtmâ) because in unbeginning and unending time He is the helper of the Kâla which is Srishti (Anâdyanante kâle srishtirûpa-kâla-sahâyât). The connection again is one between cause and its possessor. Again "friend" indicates the causality (Nimittatvam) of Kâla. For it has been said : " It has its beginning in Lava and ends in Pralaya; and is full of Tamas Shakti. Lava is the time taken to pierce with a needle a lotus-petal. Thirty Lavas > one Truti. This Kâla is Apara : for there is also Para Kâla. Kâla or Mâyâ is the cause of the occurrence of birth and destruction. Râ ·hava concludes that Prakriti and Kâla exist in even Mahâ-pralaya. But their permanence (Nityatâ) is a dependent one (Âpekshakanityatâ). For the permanence of the Purusha in which all things have their goal is alone independent (Svatanityatam).

From Shambhu was born the Sadâshiva who is the Doer of the five forms of work namely creation, preservation and " destruc-tion" favour (Anugraha) and disfavour (Nigraha). From Sadâshiva comes Isha, from Him Rudra, from Rudra Vishnu, from Vishnu, Brahmâ (v. 16.) On this verse Râghava says " It has been said before how they arise in Shabdasrishti. Here they arise in Artha-srishti.

The five Shivas are known in the Tantras as the " Five great corpses" (Panchamahâpreta). Shiva is constantly represented in corpse-like (Shavarûpa) form. This symbolises that Consciousness in Itself (Svarûpa) is actionless and inert. All action is by Shakti. Hence the Devî is in pictures imaged as standing on the inert corpse-like body of Shiva. The same notion is represented by Viparîtamaithuna, a prominent example of the use of erotic sym-bolism in the Shâkta Shâstra These Panchamahâpreta form the couch on which the Devî, Wave of Consciousness and Bliss, rests in the house of Chintâmani adorned with a garden of Nîpa trees, which is in the Island of Gems, surrounded with a grove of celestial trees, in the midst of the ocean of nectar (Ânandalaharî). This is the well-known Tantrik meditation on the heart-lotus of worship below the Anâhata-chakra. The Bahurûpâshtaka and Bhairavayamâla say " There is the supreme abode (Mandira) of Devî full of Chintâmani stones (which grant all desires). The great couch is Shiva, the cushion or mattress (Kashipu) is Sadâshiva, the pillow the great Ishâna. The four supports (Pada) are Ishâna, Rudra, Hari, and Brahmâ. On that Bed reclines ·the supreme Tripurasundarî." Hence the Devî in the Lalitâsahas-ranâma (v. 22) is called Panchabrahmâsanasthitâ. The Jewelled Island is a high state of Consciousness in that Ocean of Nectar which is the infinite all pervading Consciousness Itself. The Devî is united with Paramashiva in the Pranava; the Nâda over the Ongkâra being the couch on which is resting Parashiva in His Bindu form. A. U. M. Nâda, Bindu the five component parts of Om and the Shrîchakra Yantra are here referred to.

The supreme Paramashiva abides in Satyaloka beyond mind and matter. Shambhu presides over mind and his abode is Maharloka. Ether, air, fire, water, earth are presided over by Sadâshiva, Isha, Rudra, Vishnu, Brahmâ whose abodes' are Tapoloka, Janaloka, Svarloka, Bhuvarloka, Bhûrloka; and their centres in the human body are in the Âjnâ, Vishuddha, Anâhata, Manipûra, Svâdishthâna, and Mûlâdhâra Chakras, respectively. Kundalî Shakti manifests as the six: But notwithstanding all Her subtle and gross manifestations She remains over the same Chit and Ânanda; for the Âtmâ in its own nature (Svarûpa) as distinguished from its Powers and their products is the same in all times and places.

Turning then to the Tattvas the Shâradâ says (v. 17) that from the unmanifest Mûlabhûta (Prakriti or root of all creation) of the Supreme (Paravastu = Bindu) when subject to change (Vikriti) issued, through inequality of the Gunas, the Sâttvika Tattva Mahat in the form of the Antahkarana and Gunas.

Mahat is the cosmic Buddhi which is said to be in the form of the Antahkarana (Buddhi, Ahangkâra, Manas) for all three are implicitly contained in the first (Upachârâdubhayâtmakah), as also the Gunas which here mean the Tanmâtras of sound, touch, sight taste and smell. According to Nyâya the Gunas appertain each to each (Tattadvisheshagunâh); or according to Sângkhya Ether has one Guna, Air has two, Fire three and so forth. From Mahat was derived Ahangkâra which is threefold as Vaikârika, Taijasa, and Bhûtâdi or the Sâttvika, Râjasa, and Tâmasa Ahangkâras (v. 18), Râghava says that it is called Vaikârika because it issues from Parameshvara when his Sâmarasya with Shakti becomes Vikrita or disturbed. The Devas also are Vaikârika because produced from it. According to Sângkhya the Vaikârika nature is due to its generation from Pradhâna when Vikrita. The Vaikârika Devas are Dik, Vâta, Arka, Prachetâ (Varuna) Ashvi (two Ashvinîkumâra) Vahni, Indra, Upendra (Vishnorekâ mûrtti) Mitra (the third sun) and Ka (Chandra). These are the Presiding Devatâs of the senses (Indriya). From the Taijasa Ahangkâra were evolved the Indriyas. The five Tanmâtras and thence derived Bhûtas came from Bhûtâdi Ahangkâra.

2

* The Text and Commentary speak of the derivation of Ākàsha from Shabdatanmâtra, Vâyu from Sparshatanmâtra and so forth. But as the word Pûrva occurs, others read this as meaning that each becomes cause of what follows in association with what had gone before. Thus Shabdatanmâtra produces Ākàsha. From Shabdatanmâtra together with Sparshatanmâtra come Vâyu. From these two and Rûpatanmâtra come Agni and so forth.

The Shârada then gives the colours of the Bhûtas namely transparent (Svachchha) ether, black air, red fire, white water, and yellow earth, the Ādhâras of which are the Tanmâtra and the Gunas of which are sound, touch, sight, taste and smell. Râghava Bhatta says that it is for the purpose of worship (Upâsanâsthânam) in pursuance of Shâstra (Svashâstrânurodhena) that certain invisible things are here said to have colours (Atra keshânchit arûpi-dravyânâng varnakathanam). This might perhaps seem to suggest to some that the colours are not real. But if this be so is it correct? Ether is transparent which is no colour, black is the absence of colour. With Rûpa there must be colour. For what is colourless is formless. Form is only perceived by means of colour : and the last three Bhûtas are with form. Their colours are widely adopted. Thus in China also yellow is the colour of earth and red and white are generally assigned to fire and water, respectively. Possibly what is meant is that the colours are here mentioned for the purpose of worship : that is, the mentioning is for such purpose. Else how could the Yogî perceive them ? For it is said tâni vastûni tanmâtrâdîni pratyaksha-vishayâni (that is to Yogîs). Elsewhere it is said that ether is hollow or pitted (Sushirachihnam) air is moving (Chalanaparah) fire is digesting (Paripâkavân) water is tasteful (Rasavat) earth is solid (Ghanâ). All the universe is composed of the four Bhûtas entering into one another (Parasparânupravishtaih mahâbhûtaishchaturvidhaih) pervaded by ether (Vyâptâkâshaih).

Thus Consciousness as Shakti evolves mind and matter. The principles (Tattvas) of these are not always clearly understood. They may and indeed must be considered from the point of view of evolution—that is according to the sequence in which the limited experience of the Jîva is evolved—or from that in which they are regarded after creation when the experience of concrete sense objects has been had. According to the former aspect, Buddhi is the state of mere presentation ; consciousness of being only, without thought of "I" (Ahangkâra) and unaffected by sensations (Manas, Indriya) of particular objects which ex hypothesi do not yet exist. It is thus a state of impersonal Jîva consciousness. Ahangkâra of which Buddhi is the basis is the personal Consciousness which realises itself as a particular "I" the experiencer. The Jîva wakes to world experience under the influence of Mâyâ shakti. In the order of awakening he first experiences in a vague general way without consciousness of the limited self like the experience which is had immediately on waking after sleep. It then refers this experience to the limited self and has the consciousness "I am so and so." Manas is the desire which follows on such experience and the senses and their objects are the means whereby that enjoyment is had which is the end of all will to life. The Cosmic Mind projects its content as ideas and desires on to the gross sensual plane and there the individual mind enjoys them as such.

I may here observe that the same scheme exists in Buddhism where the root is given as Avidyâ, from which arises Sangskâra. This gives birth to Vijnâna (which is Buddhi) and then to Nâma rûpa that is an external world at first vaguely perceived. The desire to take cognisance of this gives rise to the six sense organs (Shadâyatana) namely Manas and the Indriyas. From this follows contact (Sparsha) of the sense organs with the external world giving rise to feeling (Vedanâ) called forth by such contact in the form of pleasure and pain. This experience produces Desire (Trishnâ which a recent work on the Unconscious calls Libido) for pleasant sensations resulting in attachment and enjoyment (Upâdâna), and then the individual Jîva consciousness (Bhâva) is born (Jâti) ages and dies and is again reborn until Nirvâna is attained. Throughout it is the will to life, the root of which is in Avidyâ which produces the instruments namely the mind and senses whereby enjoyment is to be had and which creatively imagines the content of its experience from out the store of past lives in past universes. True experience therefore can only be had by destroying the root which is Avidyâ. One of the tasks which yet remains to be done is to show the essential similarities of Buddhism and Hinduism instead of dwelling, as is usually done, on their differences, alleged or real. When it is fully realised that Buddhism took its birth in India and the implications necessary therein truer notions will be entertained of it than generally prevails.

An example from science has been given which illustrates the process stated. In some animals there are no specialised sense organs but when stimulus is often given to a particular part of a body that part gets specially sensitive to it and a particular organ is developed. The illustration of course assumes that objects have been already created. But in the evolution of the world similar principles come into play as those which exist after it has been evolved. The effect exists in its cause. Consciousness awakening to world experiences reaches forth and forth and as it seeks to come by recollection to its limited self, its desire evolves the instruments of enjoyment and projects the objects of enjoyment into the sensual world. This is the action of the Sangskâra operating in and upon consciousness.

Whilst however in the order of evolution 'Buddhi is the first principle ; in the actual working of the Antahkarana after creation has taken place it comes last. It is more convenient therefore for ordinary exposition to commence with the sense objects and the sensations they evoke. Matter as the objective cause of perception is not in its character as such under the cognisance of the senses. All that can be predicated of it is its effect upon these senses which is realised by the instrumentality of mind in its character as Manas. In science the notion of indestructible matter in atomic form is no longer held, for all matter it is now shown can be dissociated and the atom is dematerialised. The old duality of Force and Matter disappears, these two being held to be differing forms of the same thing. The ultimate basis is now recognised as Mâyâ or Prakriti Shakti. Matter is a stable form of force into which on disturbance of its equilibrium it disappears. Sensible matter (Bhûta) affects the experiencer in five different ways giving rise to the sensations of hearing (Âkâsha), touch and feel (Vâyu : not in the sense of all forms of contact, for form and solidity are not yet developed) colour and form and sight (Rûpa) taste (Rasa) and smell (Gandha). Sensible perception however exists only in respect of particular objects. But there exist also general elements of the particulars of sense perception. There is an abstract quality by which sensible matter (Mahâbhûta) is perceived. This abstract quality is Tanmâtra the " mere thatness" or abstract quality of an object. These are the general elements of sense perception which necessarily come into existence when the senses (Indriya) are produced. This is supersensible (Atîndriya) matter the existence of which is ordinarily only mediately perceived through the gross particular objects of which they are the generals and which proceed from them. Sensations aroused by sense objects are experienced by the outer instruments (Bâhyakarana) or senses (Indriya) whether of cognition (Jnânendriya) or action (Karmendriya) which are the afferent and efferent impulses respectively. The Indriyas are not however sufficient in themselves. In the first place unless attention co-operates there is no sensation (Âlochana) at all. Nextly as the experiencer is at every moment besieged by countless sensations from all sides ; if any of these is to be brought into the field of consciousness it must be selected to the exclusion of others. Lastly the manifold of sense or "points of sensation" must be gathered together and made into a whole. These three functions are those of Manas : the function of which is said to be Sangkalpa-vikalpa that is selection and rejection of material provided by the Jnânendriya. These sensations, to affect the experiencer,' must be made his own and this is done by Ahangkâra or "Self-arrogation ". It is then passed on to Buddhi which determines either by way of forming percepts and concepts or resolutions (Kartavyam etat mayâ). Thus all the Tattvas work for the enjoyment of the Self or Purusha. They are not to be regarded as things existing independently by themselves but as endowments of the Spirit (Âtmâ). They do not work arbitrarily as they will but represent an organised co-operative effort in the service of the Enjoyer the Experiencer or Purusha.

The Tantras speak of three Tattvas namely Âtmâ, Vidyâ, Shiva. The first includes those Tattvas of the Thirty-six which are called impure (Ashuddha) namely Prithivî to Prakriti ; the second the pure-impure (Shuddha-ashuddha) or Mâyâ, the Kanchukas and Purusha ; and the third the pure Tattvas (Shuddha) from Shuddhavidyâ to Shiva Tattva. I have dealt with the last two in previous articles and deal with the first in the present one. It is also said (see Jnânârnava Tantra XXI-1-9) that there are four Âtmâs constituting the Chitkunda or Mandala in the Mûlâdhâra where the inner Homa is made. By knowledge thereof there is no rebirth. These are Âtmâ, Jnânâtmâ, Antarâtmâ and Paramâtmâ.

The Âtmâ (Prânarûpî) which is in all creatures (Jantu) as the basis of their Prâna or vital principle is their Âtmâ. It is Hangsasvarûpî and is manifested in individual bodies by inspiration and expiration (Shvâsa, Uchchhvâsa). This is Jîvâtmâ. It is like the Âkâsha separated in a pot which when broken becomes mingled with the total Âkâsha. Jnânâtmâ is said to be Sâkshât-sâkshirûpaka. That is, it is that aspect of Âtmâ which witnesses all and by which the unity of all is known. It is thus the basis of Buddhi and all mental Tattvas derived therefrom. By 'Antar" in Antarâtmâ is meant the subtle Âtmâ of atomic dimension (Rahasyasûkshma-rûpakam-paramânu) which pervades every object. It is the "inner bodiness' (Antarangatâ) the spark of Paramâtmâ. It is the Hangsa known only by Yogîs. Its beak is Târa (Mantra Oṁ) ; its two wings are Âgama and Nigama. Its two feet are Shiva and Shakti. The three Bindus are Its three eyes. When this Paramahangsa is spread (Vyâpta) throughout creation then all Bhûtas spring up in their order (Akásha, Pavana, etc). Of these five the root is Chitta. This Hangsa Bird disports Itself in the Lake of Ignorance (Avidyâ) in the mud of illusion and infatuation (Mohapangka) which is the world. When this Hangsa becomes other-worldly (Nishprapancha) and dissolving (Sanghârarûpî) then It revdals, the Self (Atmânam pradarshayet). Then Its " Birdness " (Pakshitvâ) ceases. Then the So'hamâtmâ is established which is the Supreme Experience or Paramâtmâ.

To complete the creative process it is now necessary to resume the creation of Shabda (Shabdasrishti) from its supreme state (Parashabda or Parabrahman) through its three Bhâvas, Pashyantî, Madhyamâ and Vaikharî manifesting in bodies composed of the Tattvas above described ; for in this way the birth of the letters composing Mantras is shown. I will deal with this in the following article under the title " Garland of Letters " (Varnamâlâ), a subject of primary importance in the Tantras.

THE GARLAND OF LETTERS OR VARNAMÂLÂ.

We now speak of " Vâk "—" The Word "—a great concept of the Shâstras. Shruti says " Four are the steps measured by Vâk. The wise Brâhmana knows them. Three being hidden in the cave do not issue. The fourth is spoken by men in their speech."

The Parabindu is the Shabda-brahman : for on its differentiation arises the " unmanifest sound" (Avyaktarava) the Hidden Word from which all manifested speech and the objects which it denotes are derived. This is the state of Supreme Shabda (Parashabda) the evolution of which (Parashabdasrishti) has been shown in previous articles of this series. In its further development the existence of mind and body is assumed. This has been discussed in the account of the evolution of the objects (Arthasrishti) which Mind thinks and uttered Speech names. This Shabdabrahman as appearing in bodies is Kundalinî Shakti (Kundalinî shabdabrahmamayî). The Shârada Tilaka says (1-110-112) :

Sâ prasûte Kundalinî shabdabrahmamayî vibhuh
Shakting tato dhvanis tasmân nâdas tasmân nirodhikâ
Tato'rddhendus tatô bindus tasmâd âsît parâ tatah.

" She who is Kundalinî all pervading Shabdabrahman, produces Shakti. From this came Dhvani ; from Dhvani, Nâda ; from Nâda; Nirodhikâ ; from Nirodhikâ, Arddhendu, from Arddhendu, Bindu ; and then comes Parâ."

It will be observed that just as there is a sevenfold cosmic development, it is repeated here in the case of individual bodies. Kuṇḍalinī is Shabdabrahman, an aspect of Chaitanya or Consciousness (Chit). By Shakti is here meant Chit entered into by Sattva (Sattvapravishtâ) which is the Paramâkâshâvasthâ. By Dhvani is meant that same Chit when entered into by Sattva (Sattvapravishtâ) penetrated by Rajas (Rajo'nubiddhâ) which is Aksharâvasthâ. By Nâda is meant the same Chit penetrated by Tamas (Tamô'nubiddhâ) or Avyaktâvasthâ.* By Nirodhikâ is denoted that same Chit with abundance of Tamas (Tamah-prâchuryyâ) ;" by Arddhendu the same with abundance of Sattva (Sattva-prâchuryya). By the term Bindu is denoted that same Chit when in it there is a combination of the two (Tadubhayasangyogât). This development appears to indicate the gradual process whereby Shakti passes through subtle to more gross forms of potency until it reaches that full potency for manifestation w'ich is the Ghanâvasthâ State or Bindu in which Kriyâ exists in full creative perfection. So it is said " Moved by the strength of Ichchhâ-shakti (Ichchhâshaktibalâkrishtah) illumined by Jnâna-shakti (Jnânashakti pradîpitah)," that Shakti (Sâ shaktih) in male form (Pungrûpinî) who is the Lord (Prabhu) puts forth Her who is called Action (Kriyâkhyâm that is Kriyâshakti).

The Shâradâ then continues :—

Pashyantî madhyamâ vâchi vaikharî shabda-janmabhûh
Ichchhâjnânakriyâtmâsau tejorûpâ gunâtmikâ
Kramenânena srijati Kundalî varnamâlikâm

(Then Parâ) and then came Pashyantî, Madhyamâ and · Vaikharî Shabda. In this order Kundalî who is Will (Ichchhâ) Knowledge (Jnâna) and Action (Kriyâ) who is both Light (Tejorûpâ, and Chidrûpâ ; in Herself consciousness) and in the form of the Gunas (Gunâtmikâ, that is Prakriti) creates the Garland of Letters.

Parâ is Shabda as Parabindu and is motionless (Nishpanda). This as already explained becomes threefold and the threefold aspects from the Shabda stand-point are Pashyantî, Madhyamâ Vaikharî. Each of these are manifested forms of the Unmanifested Parabindu or Shabdabrahman. It is, as Râghava says, by shifting to another place in Her (Asyâmeva binduh sthânântaragatah) that Bindu which is Para when unmanifested and motionless is called Pashyantî, Madhyamâ and Vaikharî speech (Vâk). Parâ is in the Mûlâdhâra chakra, Pashyantî in Svâdhishthâna (and upwards) Madhyamâ in Anâhata (and upwards) and Vaikharî in the throat. In Kundalî, Shakti is subtle (Sûkshmâ) and in the form of mere Light (Jyotir-mâtrâtmarûpinî) and not an object of hearing

(Ashrotravishayâ). Thence She goes upward (Ûrddhvagâmini) and becomes Pushyantî self-manifesting (Svayang-prakâshâ) in the Sushumnâ Nâdî (Sushumnâmâshritâ). She again becomes Madhyamâ as a form of Nâda (Nâdarûpinî). when reaching the Heart Lotus (Anâhata). Then She goes upward as a mere undifferentiated " hûm " (Sanjalpamâtrâ avibhaktâ). It is She who appearing at the chest, throat, teeth, nose, palate and head assumes the form of all letters (Varna) issuing from the root of the tongue and lips and thus becomes Vaikharî the Mother of all sounds, audible to the sense of hearing (Râghava Bhatta). The same Commentator then says, citing the Kâdimata section of Tantrarâja " Under the influence of one's own will (Svâtmechchhâshaktighâtena) a high (Uttama) form of the Nâda called Parâ generates in the Mûlâdhâra as Prânavâyu (Prânavâyusvarûpatah). This when carried up by will (Ichchhâ) and made to appear in the Svâdhishthâna is called Pashyantî associated with Manas. Gradually led up by Her it is called Madhyamâ associated with Buddhi in the Anâhata. Carried still further upward it is called Vaikharî in the Vishuddha in the region of the throat. Thence it is generated as the Letters from A to Ksha through its presence at the head, throat, palate, lips, teeth, tongue (root, lip and back) nose, palate, and throat (together) lips and teeth (together) and throat and lips (together). Their Akshara-hood (Aksharatva) is said to be due to their being divided into different parts beginning with the letter A and ending with Ksha."

It is Chit-Shakti which is called Parâ that is to say it is Parâ Vâk not moved to vibration by the Mâyâ which reveals (Parâprakâshikâ mâyâ nishpandâ) on account of its bearing the reflection of Chaitanya (Chaitanyâbhâsavishishtatayâ). The vibratory states are Pashyantî and the other two (Saspandâvasthâh pashyantyâdyâh). Pashyantî which is in the nature of Bindu (Bindutattvâtmikâ) in the form of a general (that is not particulari ed) motion (Sâmânya praspandapiakâsharûpinî) which is manifested in the region between the Mûlâdhâra and the Navel (Mûlâdhârâdinâbhyantaravyaktisthânâ). It is called Pashyantî because of its being Jnâna (Jnânâtmakatvât). It is associated with Manas. Madhyamâ is in the form of the internal and external instruments (Bâhyântahkaranâtmikâ) and manifests as Nâdabindu (Nâdabindumayî). Hiranyagarbha sound (Hiranyagarbharûpinî) in the region extending from the navel to the heart (Nâbhyâdihridayântâbhivvaktisthânâ). It is associated with the Tattvas of specific ideation and so forth (Visheshasangkalpâdisatattvâ). She is Madhyamâ when Buddhi is Madhyamâ. Madhyama is middle that is " in the midst " between Pashyantî which is " Seeing " (Îkshana) and Vaikharî which is utterance. She is neither like Pashyantî nor does She proceed outward like Vaikharî with articulation fully developed. But She is in the middle between these two. Vaikharî is a form of Bîja (Bîjâtmikâ) as Madhyamâ is of Nâda (Nâdarûpinî, and as Pashyantî is of Bindu (Bindvâtmikâ). Vaikharî is manifested in the region from the heart to the mouth (Hridayâdyâ svântâbhivyaktisthânâ). It is called Vaikharî according to Râghava on account of its particular (Vishesha) hardness (Kharatva). Bhâskararâyâ (Lalitâ v. 81) derives it from Vi = very ; Khara = hard. According to the Saubhâgya Sudhodaya, Vai = certainly ; Kha = cavity (of the ear) ; Ra = to go or enter. But according to the Yogashâstras the Devî who is in the form of Vaikharî (Vaikharîrûpâ) is so called because She was produced by the Prâna called Vikhara. This is Virâtshabda that is the manifested letters which singly, or in combination, make certain sounds which are called Mantras. Strictly speaking all uttered sounds are Mantras, all uttered speech having a common origin or development : but in the more usual sense, Mantra means those letters or combination of letters which are used in Upâsanâ and Mantrayoga and are the Mantras of the Devatâs of Shastric worship. The Arthasrishti of Kundalinî are the Kalâs which arise from the letters such as the Rudra and Vishnumûrtis their Shaktis and so forth.

The root "Man" means "to think" and the suffix "tra' indicates the saving character of Mantra. Mantra is thus a power (Shakti) which is thought-movement vehicled by a vital force (Vâyu) which is revealed in speech. Shabdabrahman is all-pervading, undifferentiated Shakti, and Mantra is its particular manifestation. It is Varnâtmakashabda (Lettered sound) manifested by âkâsha caused by the contact of the surrounding air with the vocal organs, the formation of which in speech is in response to the mental movement or idea, which by the will thus seeks outward expression in audible sound. All Shabda has its corresponding Artha, for neither can be disassociated from the other. The word "Artha" comes from the root " Ri " which means to get, to know, to enjoy. Artha is that which is denoted by Shabda and is that which is known and enjoyed. This Artha is either subtle (Sûkshma) or gross (Sthûla). The latter is the outer physical object which speech denotes and the former is the Vritti (modification) of the mind which corresponds to the gross Artha : for as an object is perceived the mind forms itself into a Vritti which is the exact mental counterpart of the object perceived. The mind has thus two aspects in one of which it is the perceiver (Grâhaka) and in the other the perceived (Grâhya) in the shape of the mental impression. That aspect of the mind which cognises is called Shabda or Nâma

3

(name) and that aspect in which it is its own object or cognised is called Artha or Rûpa (Form), Shabda being associated with all mental operation. In the evolution of the universe the undifferentiated Shabda divides itself into subtle Shabda and subtle Artha which then evolve into gross Shabda and gross Artha. For the cosmic Mind projects its subtle Artha on to the sensual plane which is then a physical gross Artha named in spoken speech. Thus the subtle Shabda associated with cognition is called Mâtrikâ and the subtle Artha is the mental impression ; whilst the gross Shabda are the uttered letters (Varna) denoting the gross outer physical object (Sthûla artha).

Just as the body is causal, subtle, gross, and as there are three cosmic and individual states, dreamless sleep, dreaming, waking ; Prâjna, Taijasa, Vishva ; Ishvara, Hiranyagarbha, Vaishvânara or Virât ; and a fourth transcendent state or Turîya ; so there are three states (Bhâva) of sound Pashyantî, Madhyamâ, Vaikharî developed from a fourth supreme and undifferentiated state (Parâ). This last and Pashyantî represent the causal aspect of Shabda, for Pashyantî is the actual moving aspect of the unmoving Parâ ; Madhymâ is Hiranayagarbhashabda. This Sûkshmashabda and its corresponding Artha belonging to the subtle body (Linga Sharîra). In creation the Cosmic Mind first develops Pashyantî-shabda and Artha, and then projects this subtle Artha into the world of sensual experience and names it in spoken speech developed in the throat and issuing from the mouth. Vaikharî is Virâtshabda belonging, as well as the physical objects it denotes, to the gross body (Sthûla sharîra). This last Gross Shabda is language that is sentences (Vâkya), words (Pada) and letters (Varna) which are the expression of ideas and Mantra. Pashyantî is characterised by non-particular general movement (Sâmânyaspanda) the first undefined push of the Vâyu towards manifestation : Madhyamâ is specific movement (Visheshaspanda), the Vâyu commencing to differentiate, and Vaikharî is Spashtataraspanda that is the clear separate movements of articulate speech. Mental Artha is a Sangskâra an impression left on the subtle body by previous experience and which is recalled when the Jîva re-awakes to world-experience and recollects the experience temporarily lost in the cosmic dreamless state (Sushupti) which is dissolution (Pralaya). The Cause (Kârana) which arouses this Sangskâra is the Shabda or Nâma, subtle or gross, corresponding to that particular Artha. There is thus a double line of creation from the Shabdabrahman namely language expressive of ideas and the objects which these denote. Uttered speech is a manifestation of the inner " naming " or thought which is similar in men of all races. For this reason a thought-reader whose cerebral centre is *en rapport* with that of another may read the hidden "speech" that is the thought of one whose spoken speech he cannot understand. Vaikharîshabda however differs in various races owing to racial and climatic conditions, the physical formation of the vocal organs and so forth. But for each particular man speaking any particular language, the uttered name of any object is the gross expression of his inner thought movement. It evokes that movement and again expresses it. It evokes the idea and that idea is consciousness as mental operation. That operation can be so intensified as to be itself creative. This is Mantra-chaitanya when thought is not only in the outer husk but is vitalised through its conscious centre.

The above is but the Mantra way of saying that the homogeneous Consciousness differentiates as Shakti and appears as subject (Shabda) and object (Artha) at first in the subtle form of mind and its contents generated by the Sangskâra and then in the gross form of language as the expression of Ideas and of physical objects (Artha) which the creative or Cosmic Mind projects into the world of sensual experience to be the source of impressions to the individual experiencer therein. The natural name of anything is the sound which is produced by the action of the moving forces which constitute it. He therefore, it is said, who mentally or vocally utters with creative force the natural name of anything brings into being the thing which bears that name. Thus "Ram" is the Bîja of fire ; and is said to be the expression in gross sound (Vaikharîshabda) of the subtle sound produced by the activity of, and which is, the subtle fire-force. The mere utterance however of Ram or any other Mantra is nothing but a movement of the two lips. When however the Mantra is awakened (Prabuddha) that is when there is Mantra-chaitanya then the Sâdhaka can make the Mantra work. However this may be, in all cases it is the creative thought which ensouls the uttered sound which works now in man's small magic just as it first worked in the grand magical display of the World-Creator. His thought was the aggregate, with creative power, of all thought. Each man is Shiva and can attain His power to the degree of his ability to consciously realise himself as such. Mantra and Devatâ are one and the same. By Japa the presence of the latter is invoked. Japa or repetition of Mantra is compared to the action of a man shaking a sleeper to wake him up. The two lips are Shiva and Shakti. Their movement is the coition (Maithuna) of the two. Shabda which issues herefrom is in the nature of Bindu. The Devatâ thus produced is

as it were the son of the Sâdhaka. It is not the Supreme Devatâ
(who is actionless) who appears, but in all cases an emanation
produced by the Sâdhaka for his benefit only. The Boy-Shiva
(Bâla-Shiva) who thus appears is then made strong by the nurture
which the Sâdhaka gives to his creation. The occultist will
understand all such symbolism to mean that the Devatâ is a form
of the consciousness of the pure Sâdhaka which the latter arouses
and strengthens and gains good thereby. It is his consciousness
which becomes Bâla-Shiva and which when strengthened the full
grown Divine Power Itself. All Mantras are in the body as forms
of consciousness (Vijnânarûpa). When the Mantra is fully practised
it enlivens the Sangskâra and the Artha appears to the mind.
Mantras are thus a form of the Sangskâras of Jîvas—the Artha of
which appears to the consciousness which is pure. The essence of
all this is—concentrate and vitalise thought and will-power. But for
such a purpose a method is necessary namely language and deter-
mined varieties of practice according to the end sought. These,
Mantravidyâ, (which explains what Mantra is,) also enjoins. For
thought, words (gross or subtle) are necessary. Mantravidyâ is the
science of thought and of its expression in language as evolved
from the Logos or Shabdabrahman Itself.

It is in this sense that the universe is said to be composed of
the Letters. It is the fifty (or as some count them fifty-one)
Letters of the Sanskrit alphabet which are denoted by the Garland
of severed heads which the naked Mother Kâli, dark like a threaten-
ing rain-cloud, wears as She stands amidst bones and carrion, beasts
and birds, in the burning ground, on the white corpse-like (Shavarûpa) body of Shiva. For it is She who "slaughters" that is
withdraws all speech and its objects into Herself at the time of the
dissolution of all things (Mahâpralaya). From Her in Her aspect
of Mahâkundalî coiled round the Shivabindu they are derived.
Mahâkundalî when with one coil is Bindu, with two Prakriti-
Purusha ; with three the three Shaktis (Ichchhâ, Jnâna, Kriyâ and
the three Gunas, Rajas, Sattva, Tamas) with three and a half She
is then actually creative (Srishtyunmukhî) with Vikriti. Then with
four coils and so on to 51 She is according to the Shaktisanggama
Tantra (Utpatti Khanda, Ullâsa 1) Ekajatâ, Ugratârâ, Siddhakâlî,
Kâlasundari, Bhubaneshvarî, Chandikeshvarî, Dashamahâvidvâ
(ten coils), Smashânakâlikâ, Chandabhairavî, Kâmatârâ, Vashî-
karanakâlikâ, Panchadashî, Shodashî, Chhinnamastâ, Mahâmadhu-
matî, Mahâpadmavatî, Ramâ, Kâmasundarî, Dakshinakâlikâ,
Vidyeshî, Gâyatrî (24 coils) Panchamî, Shashthî, Mahâratneshvarî,
Mûlasanjîvanî Paramâkalâ, Mahânîlasarasvatî,Vasudhârâ, Trailokya

mohiní, Trailokyavijayâ, Mahâkâmatârinî, Aghôrâ, Samitamohiní, Bagalâ, Arundhati, Annapûrnâ, Nakulî, Trikantakî, Râjeshvarî, Trailokyâkarshiní, Râjarâjeshvarî, Kukkutî, Siddhavidyâ, Mrityuharini, Mahâbhagavatí, Vâsaví, Phetkârî, Mahâshrímâtrisundarí, and Shrímâtrikotpattisundarí (coils 51) respectively. Each coil is said to represent the Mâtrikâ or subtle form of each of the letters (Varna) and to denote the number of Kûtas or divisions in the Mant as of each of these Devatâs. Mahâkundalî coiled round the Shivabindu, as it were a mathematical line without magnitude, makes with it one point. When the time for creation comes She uncoils Herself and creates the whole universe in the form of the Letters and the objects which they denote. Having so created it She again rests as Kundalí in the root bodily centre (Mûlâdhâra) of all living creatures from which She manifests as Pashyanti Madhyamâ and Vaikharî Shabda. Man's body is called in the Tantras a microcosm (Kshudrabrahmânda) containing within itself all which is in the universe (Mahâbrahmânda) of which it is a part. The Yoginíhridaya Tantra (Sangketa 1) says that when Shakti first "sees" (that is ideates) She is Paramâ Kalâ in the Mother form (Ambikârûpâ) which is both supreme Peace (Paramashântâ) and Supreme Speech (Parâ vâk). She sees the manifested Shabda from Pashyanti to Vaikharî. The Pashyanti state is that in which Will (Ichchhâ shakti) is about to display the universe then in seed (Bíja) form. This is the Shakti Vâmâ. Madhyamâ Vâk which is knowledge (Jnâna) is Jyeshthâ. Here there is the first assumption of form as the Mâtrikâ (Mâtrikâtvam âpannâ) for here is particular motion (Visheshaspanda). The Vaikharî state is that of Kriyâ shakti (action) whose form is that of the gross universe. As the former Shakti produces the subtle letters or Mâtrikâ which are the Vâsanâ, so the latter is the Shakti of the gross letters Varna) of words and their objects. These letters are the Garland, of the Mother (Varnamâlâ) issuing from Her as Kundalî and absorbed by Her in the Yoga which bears Her name.

As the Yogakundalí Upanishad says :—"That Vâk (Power of speech or Logos) which sprouts in Parâ, gives forth leaves in Pashyanti, buds in Madhyamâ, and blossoms in Vaikharî. By reversing the above order sound is absorbed. Whoever realises the great Lord of Vâk the undifferentiated illumining Self is unaffected any word (Shabda) be it what it may." As the Hathayoga-pradípikâ (IV. 101-102) concisely says "Whatever is heard in the form of sound is Shakti. The absorbed state (Laya) of the Tattvas (Prakriti's evolutes) is that in which no sound exists. So long as there is the notion of Ether, so long is the sound (that is vibration) heard. The soundless is called Parabrahman or Paramâtmâ, "Shabdabrahman is thus the Brahman in its aspect as the cause of the manifested Shabdârtha. It is the ideating kinetic aspect of the undifferentiated Ether of Consciousness (Chidâkâsha) of Philosophy and the Saguna Brahman of worship. It is Chit Shakti vehicled by undifferentiated Mâyâ Shakti or the manifesting Godhead uncreated, unborn, eternal, evolving the changing worlds of name and form (Nâmarûpa) by its wondrous and unscrutable Mâyâ. Therefore as Chandî says "Reverence to Her Who is eternal, Raudrî, Gaurî, Dhâtrî reverence and again reverence; to Her who is the Consciousness in all beings reverence and again reverence."

THOMPSON AND CO, PRINTERS, MADRAS

www.ingramcontent.com/pod-product-compliance
Lightning Source LLC
Chambersburg PA
CBHW031439270326
41930CB00007B/778